Third World Women: Factors in their Changing Status

Jean O'Barr

Occasional Paper No. 2
Duke University
Center for International Studies

Resource materials for use at the college level.

Prepared under a grant to Duke University from the Office of Education, Department of Health, Education and Welfare.

Available from the International Studies Center, 2101 Campus Drive, Duke University, Durham, North Carolina 27706.

Library of Congress Number
76-23703
October, 1976

TABLE OF CONTENTS

PREFACE

The resource materials contained in this book are designed to assist college and university instructors in adding material on women in developing countries to the courses they teach. The materials can be employed in a variety of ways, depending on the needs, interests and background of the individuals using them.

The materials grew out of a course on women in developing societies which I teach at Duke University. After having offered the course several times, I was struck with how frequently students pointed out that the insights and understandings we were generating in class made valuable contributions to their studies in the other courses they were taking. These students stressed how rarely material on women was incorporated in any of their social science courses in spite of the fact that those courses dealt with political, social and economic conditions in the third world. I became convinced that there was now enough material on third world women generally available to enable non-specialists to utilize it in their teaching.

In the spring of 1975, under a grant from the Office of Education, Department of Health, Education and Welfare to the Comparative Area Studies Program at Duke, I began to prepare these materials for a wider audience. Professors Lindenbaum and Tinker joined Duke students and faculty as well as faculty from the six schools participating in the project grant, for two seminars on women's changing roles which were held in 1975. These seminar discussions helped me to focus on those factors shaping women's changing roles which are of most direct interest to individuals teaching courses in economics, politics, history, anthropology, and sociology dealing with developing countries.

For example, a course on Latin American politics will broaden its scope considerably by utilizing the ideas offered here on constraints to women's participation. Anthropologists will find Lindenbaum's ideas on how ideology both reflects and determines status provocative. The paradoxes modernization holds for women are important for historians, economists, and sociologists to consider in their presentations of social change. These examples underscore the fact that this book is designed to develop ideas about women which college instructors will find illuminating and which can be readily added to their presentations. It combines a treatment of these ideas with information on bibliographies and film sources to assist instructors in updating their courses.

Jean O'Barr
Duke University
April, 1976

AUTHORS

Jean O'Barr is a political scientist (Northwestern 1970) with special interests in African local politics. The author teaches a course on women in developing countries at Duke. She has written many articles and edited two collections of original essays on various aspects of African politics and women in developing societies. In addition, she is the Director of Continuing Education for the university, administering programs to assist adult women in returning to school. Professor O'Barr is well known nationally for her involvement with issues related to women.

Shirley Lindenbaum, Professor of Anthropology at the York College of CUNY, is an Australian-born anthropologist with research experience in both New Guinea and Bangladesh. She spent two years among the Fore of the Eastern Highlands of New Guinea. She then went to East Pakistan where she conducted research for three years. She has made subsequent visits to both places, most recently to Bangladesh in 1974 when she examined economic productivity and the social status of women for the Ministry of Rural Development and Co-operatives.

Irene Tinker is now Director of the Office of International Science of the American Association for the Advancement of Science. A professor of comparative government for many years, she has done field research on comparative development, administration, technological transfer and cultural change as well as on how public policies affect women in South and Southeast Asia. She was a founder of the Federation of Organizations for Professional Women serving as its president 1972-74. Under her direction the AAAS convened a seminar of experts to discuss women in development prior to the International Women's Year Conference in Mexico City, June, 1975.

CHAPTER I

INTRODUCTION

Women in the developing countries are undergoing rapid changes in the 1970s. The social, economic, and political contributions women make to their communities and nations are being altered in fundamental ways. The public and private roles[1] they play as members of household, kin, and interest groups are manifest in new forms. Members of their societies hold new attitudes toward "women's place." The self-images of women are changing. Women's changing roles were highlighted particularly in 1975, designated as *International Women's Year* by the United Nations.

This monograph presents in outline form the most important factors shaping women's roles in non-Western societies. Neither scholars nor policy makers have given much attention until recently to the vast, complex, and important subject of women's roles. Hence any discussion of women's changing roles is fraught with questions for which few reliable data are available. This essay—intended for teachers, researchers, and students from many disciplines as an introduction to the topic—raises issues and suggests their relationships.[2] It cannot, because of length and of the primitive state of knowledge, provide definitive answers to the questions posed below. These must await more research and greater sensitivity as to what "the second sex" is doing, thinking, feeling, planning.

The importance of getting what is known about third world women beyond the small group of people actively conducting research on the topic is critical. Inevitably, when a new topic becomes the object of scholarly interest, that interest is confined to the in-group researchers. In the case of research on

---

[1] By role, I mean the behaviors and attitudes expected of women as well as the image women have of themselves. See Ward (1963) for a discussion of social role as it applies to women in developing countries.

[2] I am grateful to the students in my classes at Duke who have helped me to formulate many of these interrelationships.

women, a second and more difficult barrier to widespread diffusion arises. The very legitimacy of doing research on women has until recently been subject to doubt on the "outside." This means that the very people who are breaking through historical and theoretical constraints have found it most useful (and probably most comforting) to talk mainly among themselves. Thus research on women is not widely known because its authors have tended to address themselves to each other in the face of a generally indifferent and occasionally hostile academic world. The situation is being altered as more and more scholars come to realize how narrow their perspectives have been when they exclude whole categories of people. Other academics are beginning to incorporate perspectives on women into their thinking, their writing, their teaching. The factors discussed here will hopefully facilitate that process of incorporation.

Before discussing factors conditioning women's roles, a caveat is in order. Almost without exception observers of women in the third world (most of whom are male) assume that the experiences of women elsewhere parallel those of American and European women and that the stereotypes they use in their personal relationships with women are sufficient to understand women everywhere. While there is a certain universality to the experience of being female, the variation in roles women play in other societies is much broader than western observers typically assume. I shall return to the universal themes below. Here it is important to take a basic lesson on anthropological relativism and recognize the wide variety of social positions[3] women have had at other times and in other places.

The most obvious differences center around home and children. Only recently have American women been relegated to and isolated in their homes, homes which are no longer units of economic production. Prior to the twentieth century, most American women participated directly as producers in the economies of their communities. The majority of women in the rest of the world still function as economic producers, a fact which many scholars believe accounts in large part for the influence these women have in areas of social life where American women lack it.

------

[3]I use social in its most general sense in this analysis and unless otherwise specified, it includes the economic and political. In developing countries, there is likely to be a much greater overlap of social, economic and political roles than is the case in more modernized (hence differentiated) societies.

2

Secondly, advanced western technology has made it possible for American women to sever the seemingly inevitable tie to children. These women can choose if and when to bear and rear children. The option to control one's body is limited to a very small segment of womankind, mainly upper and middle class women in America and Europe. The consequences which follow from a constant cycle of pregnancy and lactation are still the daily fare of most women around the globe. In order to think about women in developing countries, the first step is recognizing the limitations of recent American experience. Only then will it be possible to gather information on women in other countries and to build a comparative base for a discussion of the factors shaping women's roles.

Two sources are particularly helpful in challenging individuals to seek broader perspectives on women and their roles. One is a module by Hammond and Jablow: *Women: Their Economic Role in Traditional Societies* (1973). The authors begin by discussing the universal sexual division of labor, but are quick to point out that the specific tasks assigned to women vary enormously across cultures, thereby making it difficult to attribute any one set of differences (other than child-bearing and lactation) to biology. The main portion of the module is devoted to a description of economic activities—food production, the preparation of foods, housework, crafts, trade and other professions, newly introduced occupations, women's property and the economic aspects of marriage. Under each of these headings, the authors illustrate the activities with ethnographic examples, drawing comparative generalizations. They conclude their crosscultural survey by observing that "the data preclude the notion of biologically determined incapacities for *any* sort of work." At the same time they acknowledge that "this diversity of economic roles does not eliminate a universal constant of being female: Women's work is thus bounded by the domestic framework, concerned with the familial, private sectors of society. Roles within the public sphere are the province of men, and the public sphere is the locus of power and prestige." The consequences of women being relegated to the domestic sphere are discussed below.

A second source of provocative thinking on women's roles is Oakley: *Sex, Gender and Society* (1972). Oakley is interested in understanding how each culture manipulates biological differences of sex into systems of gender classifications and thereby creates and sustains a particular view of women's place. Unlike the Hammond and Joblow module, she goes beyond economic data into the biology of sex and the learning of gender roles. Oakley's treatment of male-female differences is particularly effective because of the historical perspective she brings to it. She suggests that there have been three times in modern Western history when the debate over female-male differences has peaked: in Elizabethan times when women had a great deal of equality that was being challenged by the rising commercialism; in the Victorian era when the debate over the relative worth of male and female again arose as a result of industrialization and an increase in class awareness; and finally at the present time when "traditional" arrangements are nullified by technology and by a new and more widespread awareness of how culture operates. In addition to using historical and cross-cultural data to show how gender classifications are superimposed on physiological differences, Oakley uses data from medical studies of intersexed individuals to underscore the impact of culture.

The Hammond and Jablow module as well as the Oakley book provide a perspective with which to begin a discussion of the changing roles of women in developing countries. Both works put forward the thesis that cultural variation in women's roles is very broad indeed, broader by far than recent western experience would suggest, and that as we analyze what is happening to women in situations of rapid social change we must constantly bear in mind the diversity of social positions from which these women begin their odyssey of change.

Despite the complexity of the topic of women's roles in Africa, Asia, and Latin America, it is both necessary and important to attempt an outline of factors influencing role options open to women. It is necessary because, as I shall argue below, the potential for women to suffer an adverse impact from "development" is great. It is also important because as women around the world come to demand a greater public role (and recent events suggest they are) we need to understand the conditions under which the achievement of their goals is most likely to occur.

I examine a series of ideas about women's roles in this essay. Eight propositions are offered for discussion by scholars and students interested in the women of developing countries.

1. The *Universal second class status* of women has not been satisfactorily explained although many intriguing suggestions are put forward.

2. The *Economic contribution* of women to their societies is probably the single most important determinant of their position.

4

3. In social systems where women do not have direct access to public power they follow influence strategies of: a) *manipulation* of the system sometimes working through the males they do have influence over (fathers, brothers, husbands) and/or; b) participation in *complementary spheres* of activities separate from, but often no less important than, male ones as a means for influencing system-wide policies.

4. Situations of *drastic social change* often have positive consequences for women as the histories of nationalist movements, guerilla activities, and wars illustrate. There are some situations, however, in which the reverse occurs and social change means restriction for women. *Urbanization* is one element of social change with a profound impact on women.

5. *Communist and Socialist governments* frequently make a very direct attack on women's traditional position. Attempts to alter that position become an important part of their ideology and policy. The degree to which such governments are able to effect change any more than other political systems is a point of debate.

6. The degree to which women participate in the cultural, social and economic aspects of life in modern countries is never matched with *participation in the political life* of these countries, either as elites or as ordinary citizens.

7. *Ideology* is a significant factor in sustaining cultural beliefs about proper roles for women.

8. *Development policies*, pursued by both national governments and foreign donors and agencies, may have a particularly adverse impact on women.

CHAPTER II

SEXUAL ASYMMETRY AND THE STATUS OF WOMEN

The asymmetrical social, economic, political, and ritual relations between men and women around the world are based in the complex cultural interpretations societies superimpose on biological differences. A discussion of the changing roles of women in developing countries must begin by asking how culture interacts with biology, why women's position is universally evaluated as inferior to men's, and how this evaluation is maintained today.

The basis of differentiation. Harris (1971) states the issue of how culture interacts with biology succinctly:

> Some of the most important culturally induced personality phenomena are associated with sex-linked and specialties. Since differences in the anatomy and physiology of human males and females are so obvious, it is easy to be misled into believing that sex-linked roles and statuses are primarily biological rather than cultural phenomena. Men are taller, heavier, and stronger than women, hence it is "natural" that hunting and warfare, should be male specialties. Men have higher levels of testosterone; hence they are naturally more aggressive, sexually and otherwise, and are "naturally" dominant over women. Moreover, since women menstruate, become pregnant, and lactate, they "naturally" are the ones to stay at home to care for and feed infants and children.

> The ethnographic record does indeed suggest that physiological and anatomical differences between men and women are largely responsible for certain worldwide specialties.

> 1. In all hunting and gathering societies men specialize in hunting the large game, while women specialize in small game, shellfish and vegetable products.

> 2. In all known human societies men have exercised a dominant role in the maintenance of law and order in nondomestic contexts, especially in intergroup relations.

6

3. In all known societies, the primary police-military force consists of males specially trained to use such weapons.

4. In all societies, women are the specialists in rearing infants.

One conclusion to be drawn from these facts is that the male's superior strength has conferred an adaptive advantage upon sociocultural systems that have made the control and use of weapons and instruments of the hunt and warfare a male speciality. This conclusion must not be confused with the popular notion that it is "natural" for men to be the warriors and hunters, or that it is "natural" for women to cook and take care of children. Modern anthropology has conclusively demonstrated that there is nothing purely "natural" about human hunting, warfare, political organization, or domestic life. All sociocultural practices represent the selective result of the inter-action between culture and nature. Males are not born with an innate tendency to be hunters and warriors, or to be sexually and politically dominant over women. Nor are women born with an innate tendency to care for infants and children and to be sexually and politically subordinate. Rather it has been the case that under a broad but finite set of cultural and natural conditions, certain sex-linked specialties have maximized productive and reproductive capacity, whereas the absence of these specialties or their inversion would have had the opposite effect. As the underlying demographic, technological, economic, and ecological conditions to which these sex-linked roles are adapted become modified or cease to exist, new cultural definitions of sex-linked roles may begin to emerge.

It is clear that the basic conditions responsible for the production or reproductive advantages associated with male supremacy are dependent upon the use of weapons and instruments for which human muscle power is the prime energy source. In advanced industrial contexts, the physiological and anatomical differences between male and female no longer decisively influence manipulation of the instruments of production of political-military control. Modern weaponry and industrial automation cancel out the physiological and anatomical bases of male supremacy. Most of the male-dominated specialties in agriculture, industry, government, and police-military life no longer can be said to benefit from the extra quantum of muscle power associated with the male physique. While menstruation, pregnancy, and lactation involve disadvantages in a few situations requiring rapid mobility or continuous effort

7

under stress, modern armies, governments, and corporations are already adjusted to high levels of absenteeism and frequent change of personnel. Moreover, with the long-range trend toward decreased fertility under industrial conditions, women are pregnant on the average less than three percent of their lives. Furthermore, bottle formulas have eliminated or greatly reduced the period of biologically unavoidable breast feeding (581-583).

The origins of asymmetry. The theory that biological differences dictate roles is at least convincing by itself because of the tremendous variance in roles assigned to the two sexes cross-culturally and because ultimately evaluations of the inherent worth of roles are made by people themselves, for nature does not offer judgments. The question of why women's status is universally evaluated as inferior to men's is raised with increasing frequency today, inspired by the hope of many that understanding the causes will lead to effective remedies.

Status is often defined along two dimensions, one the degree of power or authority held and second the degree of deferential treatment accorded. In studying women, however, the degree of deferential treatment accorded may be independent of, or negatively related to, their degree of power (Sanday 1974: 191). A more dependable evaluation of status rests only on the power-authority dimension. Using this definition, women's status can be shown to be subordinate to men's because, although they occasionally acquire some influence by adapting to and manipulating the structure of their particular environment, for the most part "women everywhere lack generally recognized and culturally valued authority" (Rosaldo 1974:17).

The factors causing asymmetry are numerous and complex. Recent scholars offer a variety of interpretations. Most writers begin by acknowledging the division of social life into separate spheres on the basis of sex. It is, in Janeway's words, "a man's world" in which women have a "place" (1971). Rosaldo contends that child rearing, being by convenience primarily women's work, leads to a differentiation between *domestic and public spheres.* Women carry out their lives within the confines of family and the kin-based group, the private arena, whereas men's lives are lived in the extra-kin networks or public arena. Although this differentiation does not explain how values are assigned, it does provide a basic framework for understanding how women relate to social life that becomes particularly important later in proposing remedies.

8

Socio-cultural explanations. Chodrow (1974) builds on this private-public distinction to explain the origins of the *devaluation of women's sphere.* She dismisses both biological differences and deliberate socialization as being unconvincing explanations. Instead, she proposes that the "crucial differentiating experience in male and female development arises out of the fact that women universally are largely responsible for early child care and later female socialization" (43). Both sexes of children identify with and develop an attachment to a single mother early in their lives. But young boys, in order to achieve masculinity, must break this dependency and establish an identity with men; this often is a positional, abstract identification because of the frequent absence of men from the domestic sphere. A boy comes to view masculine as that which is not feminine. This attitude, along with his denial of his initial attachment, leads him to devalue that which is feminine.

Chodorow suggests that girls' roles are immediate and involve a personal identification. Identification may be so close that a girl may have difficulty developing her own ego boundaries. Chodorow contends that while men gain societal superiority, they also guarantee themselves a permanently defensive and insecure psyche. But girls, in certain situations, gain security and a sense of worth because of their upbringing. These situations occur when full ego differentiation occurs but the girl still retains the capacity to feel open and secure with others. Chodorow, while explaining men's devaluation of women's roles, advances little toward explaining why for so long a time women seemed to have arrived at the same conclusion about their worth as did men.

Ortner (1974) handles the question of sexual asymmetry more thoroughly in her dichotomized *comparison of women/nature and men/culture.* Ortner argues that woman is identified with nature because her physiology, her social role, and her psyche set her apart from men and place her closer to the environment. Her physiology includes her unique capacity for reproduction and lactation, which duplicates the force for regeneration so ubiquitous in much of nature. Her social roles include the rearing of children—being "barely human and utterly unsocialized" (7)—which emphasizes her ties to nature. Finally, differences in temperament (thought by Chodorow to be caused by female socializers rather than by inherent physical differences) also set women apart and are used as justification for the nature analogy. Ortner hypothesizes that women's acceptance of their secondary status arises from the fact that they view the same evidence as men and consequently reach the same conclusions. Men are associated with culture partly by their lack of association with nature, but

9

also because their biological limitations dictate that they can only create artificially. Male creations must be based in human consciousness which tends to elevate the value of such creations (75).

Economic explanations. Economic explanations for the origins of asymmetry are also frequent. Sacks (1974) reworks Engels' contention on private property to demonstrate a possible social mechanism which explains the subordinate status of women. Engels argues that the presence of private property led to a decrease in the importance of the clan and increase in the importance of the family. Unlike the clan, the family unit was not egalitarian, but rather consisted of some propertyless dependents. Sacks denies that property ownership is the basis for male supremacy since many males lack private property while many females own and control private property. Sacks proposes that class societies tend to socialize the work of men and domesticate the work of women because it is most profitable for the ruling class to do so. This creates a basis for denying women full status and for defining them as wards of men. Observers of women's status in socialist countries support Sacks' ideas, a point discussed in subsequent sections.

Sanday (1974) contributes another model to this debate on the origins of asymmetry that is in some respects very similar to Ortner's and Rosaldo's; She divides traditional life into three domains: reproduction, subsistence and defense. Because biology awards women the major role in reproduction, men must undertake the bulk of subsistence tasks. As defense becomes more crucial and men assume this task because of their availability, women partially replace men in the subsistence domain. Men control the public domain outside of the localized family unit and they control resources outside of the private domain. The demands of warfare determine the division of labor within the subsistence domain which in turn determines the extent of resources controlled by women. Sanday contends that the division of labor and the amount of differentiation between public and private spheres act together to determine women's status.

Conclusion. No single explanation satisfactorily accounts for the relative devaluation of women's status cross-culturally. The important point in all the explanations is that the allocation of roles and the subsequent asymmetry have been tied in some way to the child-bearing activities of women and the ecological requirements for existence. As women are freed from an inevitable tie to pregnancy and lactation and as societal requirements for physical strength are

10

made obsolete by technology, the basis for sexual asymmetry becomes questionable. The explanations reviewed here indicate some major points of view on the origins of asymmetry. The following sections discuss the perpetuation of asymmetry and its interplay with other factors influencing women's roles. The roles women in developing countries play and the statuses they hold are a result of the interplay of many factors as the following sections amply demonstrate.

The conclusion which seems warranted here then is that while culture has reinforced biological differences in the past for adaptive reasons, the changing nature of ecological requirements in modern life negates the importance of biological differences to survival. The fact that cultural stereotypes continue in the face of the absence of an ecological base is the issue that bears discussion.

CHAPTER III

THE CONTROL OF RESOURCES

A second constant and salient theme in the literature on women in developing countries is the economic contributions women make to their societies. Around the world men and women work, playing distinct and important parts in their society's subsistence. Hammond and Jablow (1973) and Boserup (1970) survey the extent and variety of women's economic contributions. While the extent of women's work in subsistence economies is well-documented, the social consequences of playing such economic roles are less well understood. It appears to be the case that the greater women's economic contributions, the greater the likelihood that women control the resources produced and that such control over the distribution of these resources is a potential source of influence in all societies.

Friedl (1975), in an anthropological review of the determinants of sex roles, put the issues this way:

> . . . it is the right to distribute and exchange valued goods and services to those not in a person's own domestic unit (extra-domestic distribution) which confers power and prestige in all societies. It is indeed better to give than to receive. Those who work to produce goods have a greater chance to be assigned the control of distributing them, but do not automatically gain the right to do so. For the roles of men and women, this argument leads to the particular hypothesis that the prevalence of male dominance is a consequence of the frequency with which . . . men have greater rights than women to distribute goods outside of the domestic group . . . Even if women contribute their labor to the acquisition of subsistence, the chances are better than if they do not that they will have distribution rights outside of their households, but there is no assurance that they will. If, on the other hand, they do not so contribute their labor, their chances of having such rights are negligible or nonexistent (9).

The centrality of control over production and distribution to women's social status becomes painfully evident when that control is diminished. Boserup

12

(1970) was one of the first economists to point out the effects of this process. In a penetrating analysis of how the introduction of modernized systems of farming and wage labor influence women in Africa, Asia, and Latin America, Boserup documents the increasing gap in productivity between women and men. The chapter by Tinker, included in this book, details the way in which the process Boserup outlines is now being played out throughout the third world, exacerbated by Western development policy. In brief, the situation might be outlined as follows.

When the colonial powers first began interacting with the now developing countries, women were largely occupied with domestic duties and the daily work of subsistence agriculture. Particularly in Africa, where men had more leisure time, fewer previous commitments, and hence were more mobile, they were more easily coopted into the process of introduced modernization. Western occupational stereotypes with their sexist biases seemed to further the neglect of women in the development process. Promoting the idea that for women to work reflected the inadequacies of men (who were the only ones considered truly able to carry on the production), the "lazy" men were encouraged to assume agricultural tasks.

European settlers, administrators, and technical advisors were often responsible for the lowering of women's status by assuming their incapabilities. Also, in stressing cash crop farming over subsistence, Europeans introduced technology into what they helped define as the male agricultural sector, thereby reducing women's original participation in the labor force further. Men subsequently monopolized the use of new equipment and modern methods while women continued with the traditional: male productivity and status increased while that of the female decreased. In Africa, this transformed way of life brought drastic changes in status between the sexes. Colonizers in the Middle East reaffirmed the already secluded, domestic role of women. Such selective cultural "protection" and further discriminatory educational policy stimulated a productivity gap between male and female producers, eventually justifying colonial government prejudice against women farmers. Colonial legal reforms led to the loss of women's right to land ownership and changed their roles from independent cultivators to their husbands' assistants.

Colonizers were not the only factor influencing a shift from the primacy of women to men in agricultural systems. Increasing population and land use also played a part. As population pressure increases and as less land is

13

available for shifting cultivation, production becomes more settled and the plow is introduced. The resulting high intentisy use of land has meant a greater involvement of men in agriculture—and a subsequent lessening of involvement by women. Only when land pressure builds up even more dramatically do women appear to reenter the agricultural labor force as assistants in the family production unit. In the transition then from female to male oriented agriculture, women's productivity decreases and they become more dependent on men for subsistence. Rather than immediate "unemployment" however, African women adopted subordinate roles by cultivating small plots of land requiring high labor intensity techniques. Asian women, however, were simply thrust further into their domestic seclusion with the advent of the plow.

Traditionally, the sex that grows a crop has at least some of the right to trade it and control the resulting income. Development, therefore, brought not only a production shift, but also a transfer from women to men in trading activities, further detracting from the independent status of women. Extending to the industrial sphere, specialization in the production of household subsistence goods forced women out of this area of the labor force because they could no longer combine it with other domestic tasks. This loss for women was not offset by rapid recruitment into the growing modern sector as was the case with men. With industrialization came the change from a barter system to a monetary economy, where women risked being forced into even greater economic dependence on the men.

Finally, the rural-urban migration pattern introduced by the process of modernization further decreased a woman's productive role and independence (Overseas Liaison Committee, 1976). It is often assumed that women would be far better off to give up their routine, arduous role of subsistence producers in order to adopt a life of leisure in the city. Along with this, however, come lost feelings of productive worth, discrimination, and greater dependence on men. Previously, women with separate earnings had safeguards against men if they failed to support them, but this security is lost with city life. Although women are left with more time for non-domestic activities, they are frustrated by constantly closed doors to meaningful employment. Many women in urban areas express this strain between a taste of autonomy and the pull of strong traditional norms. While men formerly lived off the products of women, now the situation is reversed. Because the woman is no longer able to carry on subsistence activities within the urban setting, the family must now pay for these same goods and services—placing a financial strain on them. There is an

14

additional need for women to make productive contributions from which they are barred. With development, the structural shift in the economy reduces women's share in the total labor force. Because of a failure to find modern employment to replace former productive input, migration to the cities cuts off women from their source of employment. As a result, even though the proportion of women working in the modern sector may increase, the over-all percentage of economically active women decreases.

Boserup's analysis of the decrease in women's contribution to the economics of developing countries, plus the awareness that prior to the introduction of modern economies and their technology women had greater economic input both underscore the importance of women's economic role to her overall social status. Economic exchange has been a central factor in enhancing women's status throughout the world. Decreasing the economic options open to women results in restricted roles and lower status. An awareness of this situation is now officially recognized by government planners and foreign aid personnel. The difficulty of breaking out of this situation is also increasingly and painfully being felt by third world women themselves. However, the remedies for this negative situation are not as readily obvious because the place of women in modernization is part of a wider and more complex social fabric which is only haltingly altered.

CHAPTER IV

INDIRECT ACCESS TO INFLUENCE

Women employ strategies that can be thought of as *manipulative* and *complementary* in social systems where they do not have direct access to influence in either the public or private spheres. Most observers disregard or devalue the strategies women use to gain influence precisely because they are indirect. A reassessment of the impact of women's strategies has come about recently as feminist scholars—especially those researching women in developing countries (O'Barr 1975)—question the assumptions of their predecessors who lacked sensitivity to the roles of women in society.

Manipulative strategies are generally viewed as derogatory. Used to describe a woman whose primary means of effecting the ends she seeks is through structuring the social and physical environment around her, scholars negatively evaluate manipulative strategies. This perspective assumes that direct office-holding, overt exchange of material items, open group formation, forthright persuasion, etc., are the "desirable" ways to achieve the ends sought. However, such a perspective fails to take into account the fact that cultural systems often preclude some categories of people from direct access to power in public and/or private arenas. Hence some people cannot employ such a positively viewed, direct approach. Developing alternative and necessarily indirect strategies, as women do, becomes an adaptive, successful technique.[1]

One of the first observations made by scholars interested in women was the fact that whatever women do is seen as idiosyncratic—by both the women themselves and those who observe them. Social observers have not seemed concerned with finding patterns and regularities in women's lives. Another way of expressing the same idea is to note that the social science literature rarely views

---

[1] I am not suggesting that indirect strategies are any more or less successful than direct ones, but rather that they are frequently the only ones available to women and that they have been disregarded as insignificant for understanding social life. Even if one admits, for the purposes of argument, that they are usually a second-choice strategy, their impact is almost always ignored in analysis.

women as social actors. Rather, women are seen as objects which were acted upon (whether sexual, domestic or material). The assumption that women's behavior can be seen primarily as derivative of male behavior reinforces the view that women's activities are interesting only for what they explain about men and not for what they might illustrate about the goal directed behavior of women themselves.

Women's roles are better understood, then, if the scope of analysis is broadened to include *indirect* strategies and the patterns in them. Any strategy which assists an actor in achieving her or his ends (whether or not it is negatively viewed by the society and/or the observer—in itself a reflection of the culture's view of women) is an important variable to incorporate in understanding social processes. Women are social actors whose activities exhibit regularities in and of themselves.

A convenient way to describe how women influence their environments is to divide their strategies into three analytic categories: Manipulative, complementary, ascendant. This is the paradigm Matthiason uses in *Many Sisters* (1974), a collection of ethnographic essays on women throughout the world. "Manipulative" societies, according to Matthiason, include those in which "women feel that they are inferior to men and resort to deceit, withdrawal, artifice, or circumvention to attain their own desires." "Complementary" societies are those which value women " for themselves and the contributions they make to society. In these societies, women are neither inferior or superior to men, merely different." "An ascendant society (very infrequently found) is one in which it may be an advantage at times to be a woman. Being a woman is an advantage at times in other societies; however, the difference is one of frequency. In an ascendant society the basis of the advantages is institutionalized" (xviii). Examples of ascendant societies are rare; we do not deal with them here.

The Melanesian Lau in the Solomon Islands are one example of a manipulative society (Maranda 1974). Subject first to the authority of their fathers and later their husbands, Lau women, along with their men, believe that women are inferior. Their attitudes, their daily routines, their arrangement of their environment all support the basic assumption that higher status and prerogatives belong to men.

However, Lau women have developed mechanisms which permit them to defy the authority of men. Women can curse their husbands if they

17

are newly married and want a divorce—or if desperate—they may curse themselves. A woman can also flee to the women's seclusion area to avoid work, a beating, or consummating a marriage. A village can be thoroughly disrupted if a woman feels so mistreated that she gives birth in the village rather than in the birth hut. The village becomes polluted and the men must leave it until it has been ceremonially purified (Matthiason 1974:427-428).

In the other societies described in *Many Sisters* as manipulative ones, women employ diverse techniques to circumvent male authority and to structure social relations in ways beneficial to them. Withdrawal is a frequent technique. Women may run away from impending events; they may refuse to participate in expected activities, using socially condoned excuses for their lack of participation. Speaking indirectly, suggesting rather than telling the principals in an activity what they might do or say, is another often used technique. Yet another is to attempt to arrange their social milieu in ways favorable to them: to plant ideas, to attribute behavior, to infer that so-and-so holds a perspective, all are goal-directed activities initiated by women. The consequence of such behavior is to structure a woman's domestic arena in ways she views as advantageous.

And it is not just that she can manipulate domestic arrangements to her satisfaction: domestic relations provide the direct backdrop against which events in the public arena occur in most developing societies. Lindenbaum, discussing the formation of cooperatives in Bangladesh, in Chapter 8, shows how male reaction to government backed plans for women resulted in the failure of a development scheme. In this way, women have an indirect, but crucial, influence on community-wide social processes. Their own attempts to gain a particular daughter-in-law may upset the village equilibrium for years at a time. Their agricultural or market endeavors undergird the subsistence condition of the community. To say, then, that women are social actors who manipulate other actors in an attempt to have some control over the outcome of social dynamics adds to our understanding of how communities operate and why things happen as they do.

The idea of complementarity is one which is probably more familiar than that of manipulation to people who deal with developing countries. The literature on male-female relations frequently stresses that men's and women's spheres are quite separate and that the intra-sex interaction predominates in developing societies. This fact contrasts with the "couple front" of Western societies where the basic unit of social interaction is a woman and a man.

Dupire (1971), studying the position of women in a pastoral society, shows how complementarity operates. She says that "In Bororo beliefs, the sexes are opposite and complementary, but belong to one and the same human category which is totally different from, and excludes, all other categories" (49). "Men and women complete each other like the prow and poop of a ship, the west and east of a line on the horizon, the head and hindquarters of an animal, the blood and milk of a living creature" (50). Sex role differentiation begins early in life among the Bororo and is reinforced at each stage in the life-cycle: the emphasis in the socialization process being on the different but essential nature of each sex role. In the relations between husbands and wives, the differentiation continues. The division of labor in this pastoral society is sex-based and means that each sex pursues its own tasks during the day. "The husband eats with the men of the compound, his wife with the women and children, and each goes his or her separate way to the well or to the market" (64). Men and women have ownership rights in and control over the distribution of the products of the cattle. Dupire shows that prestige is derived from the wealth which women can accumulate and distribute, illustrating well the hypothesis put forward by Friedl that the right to control the distribution of valued resources is fundamental to women's status. The portrait that Dupire gives of women in this particular group of pastoralists suggests that while they are in legal, political, and religious spheres regarded as minors, they by no means lack independent spheres of activity culturally considered complementary and crucial to the male sphere. Within those spheres, women have discretion in structuring their lives.

Women's associations in both "traditional" and "modern" times exhibit another aspect of complementarity. Women's associations existed in traditional societies around the world as age-sets, initiation groups, secret societies, marketing groups, work groups, and cults of many varieties. Many associations for women have also emerged with social change—groups of women brought together by modernizing agents (churches, educational bodies, governments, political parties) for some particular purpose; new and old associations formed or transformed by women who are themselves touched by the process of social change and seek to regulate trade, provide social services, promote the local economy, etc.[2] Within such associations, women attempt to promote their own

---

[2]Little (1973) had written extensively about women's associations in modern urban areas of Africa. He shows how important associations are as secondary socializers for urban women.

19

interests. Not only are the associations independent of male influence and training grounds for female leaders, they can also have direct influence on the community-wide social system.

The most thoroughly documented illustration of the impact of women's associations on politics is the Aba Riots. In 1929, Ibo women in Nigeria engaged in collective and public action to protest the British colonial government's plans for taxation. Viewed at the time as frustrated sporadic protests to unpopular government measures, the women's war was said to have been won by the British who, through military action, quieted the area. Later investigations by Van Allen (1975) have uncovered a very different sequence of events and as well as a more insightful explanation for them. Van Allen shows that Ibo women, involved in at least two separate sets of complex organizations ranging over most of southeastern Nigeria, used traditionally sanctioned mechanisms to redress an externally imposed alteration in the political system. In the society of the time, women had associations of those within the same village or lineage; these associations were primarily concerned with ritual and social functions. Women also participated in multi-purpose women's groups where rules were made about crops, markets, livestock, moral norms, etc. Through these groups women could exert pressure on men to conform; males who violated the rules were subject to collective discipline. It was this collective discipline which manifested itself in the public events known to colonial officials as the women's war or riots. As Van Allen observes:

> Because the women—and the men—regarded the investigation (by the colonial government) as attempts to discover whom to punish, they volunteered no information about women's organizations. But would the British have understood them if they had? The discovery of the market network had suggested no further lines of inquiry. The majority of District Officers thought that the men had organized women's actions and were secretly directing them. The women's demands that the Native Courts no longer hear cases and that 'all white men should go to their own country'—or at least that women should serve on the Native Courts and a woman be appointed a District Officer—were demands in line with the power of women in traditional society, but were regarded by the British as irrational and ridiculous (1976: in press).

The argument then that women have multiple means to influence which may not be obvious to the observer looking for direct office-holding, overt

20

community-wide leadership, or high religious offices is amply documented in the literature on women in developing countries. This is particularly apparent when one remembers that extensive differentiation is not characteristic of every level of social organization in developing countries. Hence, the strategies women employ in general social relations impact what is more narrowly viewed in the West as communal or political.

CHAPTER V

SOCIAL CHANGE AND THE ROLES OF WOMEN

Situations of rapid social change in the developing countries have a variety of consequences for women. No single generalization is possible because the nature of the changes varies greatly as does the extant positions of women in different cultures. Radical social change often has positive consequences for women. The histories of nationalist movements and guerilla warfare supply evidence for this hypothesis. In situations in which there is a general upheaval of the social structure, old conventions about who does what may become inapplicable and opportunities for women to play public roles may appear for the first time. In other situations of intensive social change, the reverse may occur. The social system may respond to change by rigidifying patterns of male and female relations. In still other cases, social change can operate more insidiously, either breaking down some of the most restrictive aspects of the old culture for women or removing many of the prerogatives guaranteed women under the old system. The consequences of social change for women's roles are then as diverse as the situations in which women find themselves (Gordon 1968). The factors underlying various types of reactions can be seen by exploring several instances of intense social change.

Women in nationalist movements. African women played a central role in the nationalist movements in that continent from the end of the 1940's. The women of Guinea provide a prototype of such involvement. When Sekou Toure became Secretary General of the Democratic Party (PDG) in 1948, he addressed his appeals for change under the French colonial regime to three groups he defined as particularly alienated by the status quo: wage earners, urban youth and women. Toure believed that women had the most to gain from radical social changes. French colonial policies meant that Guinean men were regularly taken off into forced labor, thereby violently disrupting normal familial and community relationships, and that women, as holders of rights and obligations under traditional systems, were systematically denied them under colonization. Organizing women in the PDG became one of the major activities of the early nationalist period. In 1951 women voted for the first time in Guinea and overwhelmingly gave their support to Toure and his party. Dobert (1970) reports the following incident of the period:

22

Women also justified Toure's faith in them by collaborating in the famous strike of 1953. This strike, begun on orders from the head-quarters of the General Confederation of Workers (DGT) in Paris, lasted ten days in the whole of French West Africa, and for 73 days in Guinea, and seriously weakened the colonial government. While it continued, women traders refused to sell chicken, eggs and fresh milk to the French and fed strikers without payment, and peasant women collected rice as their contribution.

Macire Sylla, a peasant woman from the region of Telimele, provides a good example of women's attitudes at the time. She recalls carrying water to people attending secret political meetings in the bush, and during the June 1964 elections, when tensions between the country's French-backed conservatives and Toure's followers exploded in fierce street brawls, she collected rocks in her shawl and carried them to the men who threw them at French soldiers. She herself was hit by a rifle butt which knocked out her teeth (26-27).

Not only were African women direct participants in many of the nationalist activities—they fed into the numerous local grievances which the nationalist movements coopted throughout the continent. African nationalist movements continually incorporated local groups and events into a larger struc-ture. The women of Pare District in Tanzania provide such an example (O'Barr 1970). In 1942-43 the District Council, composed of nine Native Authority Chiefs, levied a new tax. The tax was for development purposes, but was to be assessed using a traditional basis (presumably to enhance its popular accepta-bility). Opposition to the tax arose among the new elites—the teachers, the clerks, the traders—who foresaw the beginnings of a graduated income tax and who questioned the right of the Native Authority Chiefs to represent them. Dis-cussions between the various groups stymied. Early in 1945, thousands of men from throughout the district marched on the district headquarters and an-nounced their intention to remain until the tax was abolished.

After several months of demonstrations and no progress in discussions, the women of one of the sub-districts also marched on district headquarters. They presented themselves as a delegation to the British District Officer, said they supported the position their husbands, fathers, and brothers were taking. The women demanded that the DO impregnate them if he refused to effect a settlement and allow the men to return to their homes and their farms. The women claimed that the controversy over taxes had so disrupted the normal life-cycle that their society was collapsing. They argued that if the DO forced the men to abandon their wives and their work, he was responsible to substitute for the men, even to the point of impregnating the women. Shortly after this confrontation, the provincial governor and representatives from the territorial government were stoned by crowds of women when they toured this same subdistrict. Believing that the situation had taken on new and uncontrollable dimensions with the women's mobilization, the Native Authority Chiefs, with the consul of the DO, relented and the tax was dropped. This episode was the beginning of the Pare protest movement which Nyerere's TANU later incorporated in the sweep to independence.

These two examples illustrate situations in which women are mobilized by emergent authorities as a new base of support. In these cases social change can be viewed as opening up new options for women with potentially positive consequences.

Guerilla warfare and women. African women's contributions to the nationalist movements are not the only examples of women playing new and direct political roles in situations of rapid social change. Accounts of the Palestinian refugees show much the same pattern. Although the social change experienced by the refugees does not have the positive, progressive overtones frequently associated with the term, the situation in which they find themselves is a fundamentally altered one. The refugees are not, of course, participants in a nation-state system by virtue of their status. But certain developments in the position of women in that society reflect the way social change creates conditions in which women take new initiatives.

Since the 1967 Arab-Israeli War, the role of Palestinian women in political activities within the refugee camps themselves has steadily increased to the point where women now form the nucleus of the resistance. They are the principal leaders of civilian demonstrations in occupied territories (Israel) and they actively participate in the national liberation movement, Al Fatah, engaging in guerilla raids, functioning as liaison officers for the underground network, hiding guerillas, raising funds for the movement, and proselytizing the liberation cause.

This is by no means a new avenue of participation. Rather it is one that has been rediscovered by Palestinian women of late. As far back as 1919 women were involved in a protest against the British rule over Palestine. In the 1936 revolt, women led demonstrations, carried guns and supplies to the men and even, in isolated cases, were said to have fought and died against the British. The armed conflict with Zionists in 1948 saw the organization of a women's volunteer division to help in the cause. In each instance, women were temporarily freed from the traditional Islamic restrictions on their public activities and had contact with men in the name of liberation. Observers note that portions of Palestinian society, far more than any other Islamic society, have recently become radicalized as a result of their extreme political situation. That is, they are rejecting traditional ways and values and accepting new approaches that are required in their liberation struggle. These new approaches to the political and military problems of the refugees go far to improve women's role in public life. With a growing percentage of men working in distant places, women must be relied upon to fill the ranks of the movement (Aruri 1972:48).

The urgent and volatile circumstances which have been brought on by the political situation demand that cultural values be modified so as to permit women to participate in roles traditionally reserved for men. For example, militant meetings are held at night for security purposes and often run into the early morning hours as strategy and logistics are formulated. This creates a dilemma for women active in the movement in that "respectable" girls are expected to be home at early hours. Initially, meetings were adjourned or held at great risk at earlier hours to protect women members from being stigmatized by society or suspected by officials. But, "as the struggle intensified, political and social consciousness improved and duties piled up," it became obvious that important meetings could not be hampered by traditional social values. Young women appealed to their brothers who were also involved in the resistance movement to persuade parents and neighbors to abandon archair norms. One participant said:

As expected the brothers suffered at first from a divided soul. On the one hand they were still under the impact of the traditional role of the male as the protector of the virtue and honor of the family. But on the other hand their loyalty to the movement, to the cause, and to the exigencies of revolutionary work drove them in the direction of wanting their sisters to participate fully in the struggle.

The extreme political and military situation of the Palestinians also had a radicalizing effect on the population and fostered a new cognizance of the consequences of oppression. These elements have led to the realization that within their own society, they are oppressed by Islamic tradition. This new awareness

25

and the need to form a unified resistance movement have stimulated new opportunities for women in public life; in Al Fatah no distinction in rank or assignment
is based on gender. Women's participation in Palestinian society is enhanced because large numbers of men are out of the local environment, leaving women to
fill the gaps; because traditional values have been circumvented to accommodate
the pragmatic demands of the struggle for liberation; and because unity is required in the resistance movement if success is to be achieved. Finally, in that
political participation is the only readily available means by which to gain a
modicum of prestige, political participation has inflated the role of women in
public life in Palestinian society beyond what we might expect in societies where
an extreme political and military situation is not present and other avenues of
participation are more plentiful yet less vital.

Negative reactions to change. The consequences of extensive social
change are by no means always as positive as the above examples suggest. The
impact of colonialism on some developing countries has had the effect of both
introducing new options while at the same time causing many people, especially
men, to adopt conservative attitudes in a protective reaction. Many observers
have suggested that men alleviate the anxieties they experience either under the
degradation of colonial regimes or the tensions of modernizing governments by
reinforcing the older patterns of woman's place. For these people, change means
stricter adherence to the status quo rather than adoption of new opportunities.
Vinogradov (1974) describes such a situation for Moroccan men.

> The relationship between men and women, especially in their roles of
> husband and wife, is an uneasy one in Morocco. It is marked by a
> mutual lack of trust, by anxiety, and by a large measure of hostility.
> Moroccans complain about the high bride price, marital instability, and
> widespread prostitution. I am not arguing that these problems origin-
> ated with the colonialism; however, I do feel that they were exacer-
> bated by colonial attitudes and the effects of colonialism on Moroccan
> society. A proper study of the role and status of women in Morocco
> today must take into account the effects of French colonialism on the
> psychosexual and social relationships between men and women, by no
> means an easy subject . . . Meanwhile, it is obvious that the traditional
> Islamic ideology of masculinity and feminity and their "natural" rela-
> tionship has become obsolete in the context of today's Morocco. But,
> as yet, no new ideology has evolved to replace it; what does exist is an
> uneasy compromise between the old rigid values and the demands of

the current state of affairs whereby men and women continue to improvise their roles and strategies. Residual traditionalism dies hard, though, and the Moroccan women may have to bear the male's search for identity and self-esteem. She is already faced with the dilemma expressed by a Moroccan friend of mine. When I asked him why he was still unmarried at 35, he replied, "It is difficult to find a wife in Morocco. The majority of our women are stupid and ignorant, and the few that are educated are not feminine" (198).

The trade off in social change. The effects of social change on women involved in nationalist movements and guerilla warfare appears to mean greater opportunity for public participation in many cases. The consequences of less drastic social change are much less clear cut, as the Moroccan case suggested. Urbanization too has often produced mixed blessings for women in developing countries. Not only do women lack the educational and job skills to compete successfully in the urban environment (see the discussion in Tinker's chapter of this gap in education), but people often view the urban center as the nucleus for the breakdown of the family and attempt to protect their women from the influences ghat might be found there. Van Allen (1974a) has suggested that modernization means more dependency for African women. The African urban women have the most access to the supposed benefits of modernization, especially since most women with any education leave their villages for the towns. There, it is assumed, they are more "free" because they are no longer burdened with heavy physical labor and traditional restraints. Yet, the unmarried urban women live more economically precarious lives than their village sisters. Most have no access to jobs and therefore turn to either petty trading, illicit brewing, or prostitution. Urban wives enjoy more economic and social security than the unmarried women, but at the expense of increased dependence on their husbands. The uneducated are excluded from wage labor, not only because of the general preference for hiring men, but because most husbands fear that sex liaisons will occur if their wives work under the supervision of men. Thus, these women are in an economic bind; they are separated from their farms and still are expected to provide food for themselves and their children. The urban wives have lost not only their economic independence, but also the collective female social and political life as well. There are indications that even the educated urban women, in spite of their abilities to pursue a career, do not work after marriage. They are expected to devote their lives to the husband's career and the raising of children.

The way in which women are affected by change varies enormously. The process of change itself is uneven at best. There is some evidence to suggest that radical social change so fundamentally alters the social structure that women have new options. Likewise, some cases show that in situations of more limited change, societies rigidify in response to challenges or that women experience a trade-off at best. There seems to be no question that sex roles are one of the aspects of a culture most resilient to change and that permanent alteration in the roles of female and male only occurs when women themselves become a self-conscious group, monitoring and directing the changes they experience (Jaquette 1974).

CHAPTER VI

WOMEN UNDER COMMUNIST AND SOCIALIST REGIMES

A widely debated issue in any discussion of women's changing roles in developing countries is the effects of revolutionary regimes on the status of women. Communist and socialist countries almost always make direct attack on the traditional position of women a top policy priority.[1] Because of this some observers claim that women are more likely to realize full equality under these political systems than under any other type. Others claim that the regimes desire for change in women's status is only temporarily, though often effectively, given priority. They claim it lasts only as long as there is a need for female labor and/or as long as appealing to women brings additional support to the regime in question. These observers assert that when policies in regard to women coincide with other, higher priority goals, women's position is changed, advanced, modified. But when the goal of advancing women conflicts with other goals, they contend, it frequently falls by the wayside.

Similarly, still other observers state that change, initiated from the top in revolutionary regimes, can vastly increase opportunities or options, but that it cannot easily nor does it usually manage to change basic popular attitudes. Hence, many of the proposals for change meet resistance, at the bottom, from men and women alike.

Differing perspectives on the consequences of revolutionary regimes for women were well documented in the claims made by the delegations from Cuba and the Soviet Union during the Mexico City meeting for International Women's Year in June, 1975. The Cuban delegation claimed that their government had done more to advance the position of women than any other. In one sense their evaluation was accurate. In addition to high level policy statements and the

---

[1] I am treating both types of regimes together in this general essay. The important theoretical and empirical differences between Communist and Socialist ideologies as well as among countries practicing each are acknowledged. See Rowbotham (1974) for a history of women and resistance movements from a Marxist perspective; see Scott (1974) for an Eastern European case.

creation of many societal supports for working women, the Cubans have begun programs to try to deal directly with male attitudes toward changes for women. Admonitions for males to assume new activities in the domestic sphere—and not just for the regime to provide these services outside the family unit—are more frequent in Cuba than elsewhere. The Soviet Delegation claimed that Soviet women had advanced more than any others in the world; they pointed to statistics on education and employment which show Soviet women in a favorable light. This assertion was noisily rebuffed by other delegations who pointed to the low numbers of women in political positions in the Soviet Union, in spite of their economic and educational achievements, and the severe strain of the dual career load that Soviet women carry. In the Soviet Union, these critics say, little has been done to relieve women of their homemaking responsibilities and Soviet men are among the least changed of all men.

These claims and counterclaims illustrate clearly the controversial nature of the issue. There is little doubt that significant portions of public policy in communist and socialist regimes are addressed to the issues of equality for women; whether the reality matches the rhetoric, whether change can be initiated from above, how dependent a change in women's status is on other policy goals remain open questions (Jancar 1974; Lapidus 1974). A brief overview of the situation of women in China, the Soviet Union, and Cuba amplifies some of these issues.

The Chinese and Russian Experiences. In both the Chinese and Russian revolutions, efforts were directed not just at changing the political system but at transforming society. Both attempted to mobilize heretofore unpoliticized groups and to eliminate the old social structure. Changing the position of women was thus central to both revolutions. There is little argument that women played more prominent public roles in the revolutions in China and Russia than they had in either country in prerevolutionary days. One can find many examples in each case of women playing key parts in policy-formation and implementation as individual political actors. Such political incumbency stands in stark contrast to their pre-revolutionary roles. Furthermore, in the period of consolidation after the success of the revolutions, the need for women in the work forces of both countries meant that all sorts of institutional barriers to women's assumption of greater economic activities were changed. Greater training and educational opportunities, the provision of child care services, the equalization of pay as an incentive, encadrement were initiated by regimes, along with some coercive measures, to bring women into the work force. And the results were clearly spectacular by pre-revolutionary or cross-cultural comparisons. But with some stabilization of the economy and the countervailing pull of priorities in both systems, the advancement of women's position toward total equality with men is frequently compromised.

Leader (1973) has looked at the emancipation of Chinese women, tying party definitions of women's roles to party needs from 1950 to the present. Initially, the all out effort to get women into the labor force meant denying any differences between men and women. As resistence to such a policy arose, a new line developed whereby women's roles were defined as separate from, but just as important as, men's. Leader concludes:

> The CCP has deliberately sought to uproot women from traditio al marriage customs and family life in order to recruit them for social mobilization and political activity. At the same time, the party has tried to prevent women from creating their own new beliefs and commitments: Liberation from the past might mean the liberation of women's sexuality. Instead, the party has sought to guide women into stable marriages in which the party hopes that its authority will supersede patriarchial authority, and where work commitment takes precedence over family responsibilities. The party has clearly sought to avoid the inter mediate stage of hedonism which tends to occur after old commitments have eroded and before new ties are formed. In a developing society, where labor-intensive modes of production are the key to economic success, hedonism is the enemy of self-sacrifice and hard work.

Although Mao-Tse-Tung has consistently emphasized the importance of women as a revolutionary force and as a vast reserve of labor, he has viewed the emancipation of women as a subordinate but integral part of the broader revolutions in China in the spheres of economic, political, and cultural life. Consequently, party policy on women has always been subordinate to economic and political priorities.

Mao insists that women really are no different from men and can, if motivated, perform the same work. Therefore his policies tend to emphasize the participation of women in labor and in political work. Women, if allowed to take their place in socialist activities, will demonstrate their capabilities and thereby lose their inferiority complexes and gain equality with men.

31

However, Mao has found that sexist beliefs and values persist in the face of economic, social, and political change. Constantly adjusting theory to the unfolding reality, the party has been forced to alter its conception of the source and nature of sexism and now predicts that women will be truly equal only in the period of full communism. In other words, a meaningful liberation for women cannot be imposed from above (78-79).

Salaff and Merkle (1971) reach a similar conclusion in their comparative essay on Chinese and Soviet women. Having reviewed the ideology of the revolutions and the place of women in the early leadership, they then go on to compare the Russian and Chinese efforts to get women to enter the work force and the problems involved in providing support services on the domestic front. They say:

> The crumpling of the old regime creates a potential for women's liberation which cannot exist in prerevolutionary society. To the degree that women are oppressed by the same structure of authority that also keeps men in their place and maintains the traditional government (such as lineage systems or village hierarchies), revolutions that attack these forms of social authority will tend to liberate women. Likewise, when the conditions which suppress women can be attributed to exploitive traditional economic structures, then revolutionary efforts to change the economic system will also liberate women. Thus, in the Russian and Chinese cases, the revolution, as it broke apart the old order, freed women, primarily by removing the legal restrictions which bound them to the family and kept them from participating in production.

> But women's participation is not simply a result of general social and economic oppression; it is, in addition, a special form of oppression resulting from the unique conditions which affect women alone of all social groups. The oppression of women inheres in the most intimate, private areas of life, pervades cultural tradition and historical experience, and profoundly benefits both economically and psychologically those who women serve. Thus, it is in the interest of the revolution to liberate women to the extent that this liberation helps to destroy the traditional social structures which support the old regime. But this process will stop short of the additional effort required to liberate women from their special oppression. The costs are too great. One of the major

32

reasons that the post-revolutionary regimes in Russia and China have not been willing or able to make the effort required to liberate women fully is that both societies have suffered from pressing economic scarcities. In both cases, attempts to change the position of women were eventually blocked when they became too costly in terms of either direct economic costs such as child care and household services or political resistance and disruption resulting from attempts to change the family or to bring women equally into production. It may be that women have a better chance for liberation in revolutions which set traditional societies on the path of modernization.

In Russia and China, two special forces worked for women's emancipation: the feminists themselves and the revolutionary ideology which they only in part had influenced. The feminists, a small group of very competent and militant women, fought primarily for the liberation of women within the context of a new and free society. The revolutionaries insisted that the liberation of women was a necessary part of the revolutionary transformation creating that new society. The conflict of these forces with the political and economic exigencies of the revolutionary regimes led to a most curious synthesis: the liberation of women remained a central ideological premise in both revolutions even when attacks on basic oppression of women in the family and their inequality in and political life were lessened. Simultaneously, a "star system" with the double advantages of co-opting the minority of active talented women and providing propaganda support for the ideology of women's liberation came to absorb the energy of the feminists' drive for the emancipation of all women. Despite the crucial symbolic role played by feminist revolutions and the importance of the ideology of the women's liberation even now, the outcome has been clearly a system in which individual women are elevated as symbols of the fulfillment of revolutionary promises rather than a substantial commitment to end the oppression of women as a category. This post-revolutionary synthesis appears to result from the fact that women were not organized as a class during the revolutionary period. A militant minority, primarily from privileged bourgeois or aristocratic backgrounds, pressed the demands of women in general, but women were not united in their pursuit of equality during the revolutionary period. Because women did not form a definite power bloc, neither the revolutionary feminists nor the ideological commitment to women's emancipation were powerful enough to maintain the impetus for change when the costs became high.

33

The inevitable conclusion produced by study of these two major social revolutions is that, given the many obstacles to liberation and the conflicting demands of different oppressed groups during the revolutionary period, women must win and hold power itself during this flexible transition phase. Legal or even substantive changes in women's position cannot replace the necessary ability to enforce their interests even in the face of rival interests and demands. In particular, women in Russia and China, despite their heavy contribution to the revolution, never gained control of the means of coercion—armed force—which guaranteed their power. In addition, they did not develop mass political power or political leverage through the control of key positions in the economy, party or state apparatus. Without a power base, the demands of women were met only when their liberation was beneficial to the political and economic interests of the revolutionary regime (190-191).

The Cuban Case. The changes which revolutionary regimes bring to women's place have perhaps gone further in Cuba than under any other regime precisely because the Cuba regime has not been faced with having to decide among priorities. To date, equalization in the status of women and the country's economic and political needs are considered to be synonymous by the leadership. In addition, the Castro government has stimulated the growth of a widespread and influential women's organization, the Federation of Cuban women (FMC). The growth of the FMC has no parallel in either China or the Soviet Union and represents a militant political counter force should the regime ever begin to distinguish between woman's needs and those of the country.

Cuban policy calls for a new social order in which egalitarianism and women's equal political participation are viewed as the twin goals of the revolution. The new society is to be built on a philosophy of "humanismo" and comradeship which did not distinguish between male and female as such; all people who are sufficiently trained through equal educational opportunity are to have the chance to seek out meaningful employment so they could make a contribution to the revolutionary struggle. Women's quest for political power is to be manifested in a revolution within a revolution—the struggle to establish political mobility for women within the structure of the revolutionary movement for the whole of Cuba.

Early on, Castro, like the Soviet and Chinese leaders, equated the liberation of women with the revolution of society. "What must concern us as revolutionaries is that the work of the Revolution is not yet complete . . . the day has to come when we have a Party of men and women, a leadership of men and women, and a State of men and women, and a government of men and women" (1974:16). In the guerilla struggle against Batista, he was impressed with the power and courage of the women as exemplified by their action as guerilla leaders and aides. In an address to the Federation of Cuban Women (FMC) in 1966, he told the conference that "if we were to ask ourselves what is it that is the most revolutionary part of the revolution, it is, to say, the revolution that is taking place in the women of our country."

Because change in Cuban society is directed from above, both the rate and scope of change is determined by the Cuban government (Purcell 1973:259). Therefore, most of the changes that affect Cuban women are directly related to those goals of the revolutionary government. The major scope of these aims has been to educate the populace into a new type of consciousness that emphasizes the new "Cuban man", based on comradeship and a sense of personal being. This is the major goal of the Cuban government, for it is in constant struggle with the cultural and social traditions of years of Cuban exploitation and male superiority.

Cuba's attack on the cultural conventions which undergird the social patterns of male and female relations has led to some deep resistance among men. Fox (1973) in a very sensitive analysis of male reactions to the emphasis on women's liberation in Cuba finds such resistance. He cites several factors which lead him to believe that the changing patterns of women's activities will prevail.

Conservative attitudes like those found by Pitt-Rivers among the villagers of Andalusia are present as well among the Cuban emigre workers although modified by the heritage of black slavery and other influences. Among the attitudes common to Andalusians and the Cuban respondents is the conviction that men are naturally more aggressive sexually than women—one married woman interviewed said explicitly that a man could not be satisfied with one woman, and outside the inview setting it was clear that many, if not all, the men believed this as well—and that women are relatively defenseless against this agression without the protection of husbands or fathers. The readiness of men to talk about sexual morality with a stranger and in front of their wives, and of women to male interviewers, is at variance with the Andalusian cult of sexual secrecy that seems to be implicit in Pitt-Rivers' study. Another difference is that Cubans have many adjustments of the moral code to necessity, such as permitting women to take certain kinds of "honorable" employment outside the home. Since Pitt-Rivers was constructing an ideal type of sexual code, he did not seek to describe individual variations; it is apparent that in Cuba as elsewhere, values can be much modified in practice.

But the plasticity of conservative values is limited and those expressed by the emigres in the sample are ultimately incompatible with the mobilization of womanpower in Cuba. Overwhelming all other reactions to women's role in the new Cuba is the workers' chagrin that women are now working in agriculture. Women's activity in the Committees for the Defense of the Revolution, in the militia, in the Federation of Cuban Women and other new "mass organizations" is also threatening to these men. Since it would not be possible for the revolution to reverse itself in these areas (for one thing, the integrated women would not permit this), Cuban men must either accept the changes or they must break with the revolution. And this is not only a problem of the emigres. As a young Cuban told Elizabeth Sunderland in 1967: "The changes have been traumatic for Cuban men . . . . The hard thing is that they cannot legitimately oppose the changes. A woman who goes to work or on guard duty is doing it for the revolution. The men would have to be counter-Revolutionaries to oppose it." What I have tried to demonstrate in this paper is that accepting the new norms is no simple matter for Cuban men. It means reevaluating and ultimately rejecting their ancient code of honor and shame, which is to say their whole definition of the meaning of manhood. The old system of values is in some ways oppressive of men, both because it raises sexual frustration to an art form and because it limits men (as well as women) to only certain behaviors and styles while tabooing others. Nevertheless, Cuban men are reluctant to relinquish the elaborate code which preserves their fragile *dignidad.*

But there is another element of the honor-and-shame code that does fit the image of the "New Man" in Cuba. This is the stress on male assertiveness, long frustrated by class and colonial oppression. The New Man, the revolutionary Cuban, is supposed to shape his own and his country's destiny and in fact is doing so. This is the main meaning of men's liberation in Cuba.

36

The new generations in Cuba will be learning new skills, an instrumental rationality with regard to technology, an appreciation of the effectiveness of cooperation and *emulacion* over and against the isolated, individual effort glorified as *dignidad*; they will be growing up in a world where the important concept is not *decencia* but *concencia*, not refraining from evil but seizing a task, comprehending it, and carrying it out. For those brought up the old way, these are difficult changes (291-292).

In the three countries briefly examined here, it is clear that when revolutionary regimes call for economic progress and political control they must rely heavily on the economic and political recruitment of previously immobilized women for success. The extent to which any of the regimes has a basic commitment to equality for women outside of the primary economic and political goals is open to question. Cuba appears to have engendered greater change in women's status than the other two countries in two ways: a strong women's organization has grown up in Cuba which increasingly socializes women to new norms as well as articulate demands; Cuban policy directly attacks conceptions of male roles, a subject not mentioned in Chinese or Soviet policy.

These illustrations suggest that Communist and Socialist systems are faced with many of the same issues as other political systems vis-a-vis women, namely how to account for the lack of political roles women assume irrespective of the differences in their economic or social roles. The following section deals directly with that question.

CHAPTER VII

WOMEN'S PARTICIPATION IN POLITICS

Research on women in political science. Political scientists are just beginning to investigate women's participation in politics whereas other social scientists—anthropologists, sociologists, economists, historians—began to examine some aspects of women's roles several years ago. The political issues of interest include what accounts for the relatively low politicization of women generally, what causes somewhat higher levels of activity among women in certain countries, how and why established patterns of participation give way to new as well as why political scientists themselves rarely analyze women as political actors.

The invisibility of women in the literature of political science stems from several interrelated causes which I have discussed elsewhere (O'Barr 1975). Briefly restated the argument is as follows: Political scientists bring certain pre-conceptions, or assumptions, to their analyses of colonialism, nationalism, the events surrounding independence in the third world, and the political instability and economic difficulties experienced by developing countries. The view of social life generally taken in political science does not define women's activities as relevant for analysis. Political scientists often assume, for example, that politics can be neatly separated out from other aspects of social life. In the diverse societies now incorporated into developing countries, this may not be so. Non-state forms of political organization may predominate (Lebeuf 1971). Role differentiation and specialization may be relatively limited. Politics, economics, ritual, and social life may be fused into a single whole. The control and socialization functions most commonly designated as political ones in the West are conducted by and through non-political structures elsewhere. Thus, political scientists tend not to examine the "non-political" roles women play and consequently do not see the "political" consequences of "non-political" activities in societies where politics are fused with other aspects of social life. This approach tends to ignore women and to make their political roles invisible.

A second assumption, following closely from the first, is that politics (defined as goal-setting and seeking by means of influence and/or coercion) occurs only, or primarily, in the interaction of individuals and public authorities. In chapters three and four above I suggested that control over distribution of valued economic resources and indirect influence strategies were often used by women. In developing countries the line between public and private is not neatly drawn. During the colonial period as well as after independence, when governments made new demands and imposed rules, the public-private distinction was blurred if not obliterated. Political strategies are processes which operate universally, not just in the public domain. When treated as such, women enter the political picture more fully.

A third assumption political scientists make which limits their ability to view women as political actors is that because women universally are subordinate to men in status, the roles they do play are of little consequence in the political arena (as conventionally defined). Playing subordinate roles is not equivalent to playing no role at all! From the foregoing discussion it should be clear that women influence political life in myriad ways other than just being voters and incumbents of major political positions.

Fourth, and finally, political scientists who tend to think in terms of nation-state paradigms and are not aware of the political organization of non-state societies, are generally unfamiliar with the wide variety of political positions women have held in other times and under other conditions. The anthropological evidence suggests that women in many precolonial societies had more extensive political prerogatives than they do now under contemporary arrangements.[1]

Women as political actors. The lack of research on women's participation in politics can, thus, be explained to some degree by the perspective of the discipline. But even if the definition of politics is broadened to include women, questions about women as citizens, as voters, as members of interest groups, as incumbents are largely unexamined. Women constitute only a tiny fraction of the political leadership in any country. No matter what form the political system takes, no matter what level of education women have, no matter what their traditional status was nor what their present patterns of employment in the

---

[1]Many recent collections substantiate this observation. See Jacquette (1974), Iglitzin and Ross (1976), Leavitt (1975), Matthiasson (1974), Paulme (1971), Pescatello (1973), Rosaldo and Lamphere (1974), Raphael (1975), Ward (1963) and Wipper (1972) for ethnographic descriptions and comparative analyses.

modern economy are, women do not play major political leadership roles. Occasionally prime ministers or salient personalities suggest that in a particular country the situation may be different. But closer examination reveals that "stars" do not alter the pattern: women rarely assume conventional political roles other than voting.

The research on political behavior contains accurate predicators of what causes people to become politicized. Presumably women too will be politicized under certain conditions. Education, work experience, group membership, certain personality characteristics are the factors most frequently cited to explain why people engage in political activities. Women everywhere lag behind men on each of these indicators. Worldwide, their educational opportunities are fewer and narrower. Worldwide, they cluster in certain occupations which are an extension of their maternal concerns; in all occupations, they predominate at the lowest range. Lacking education and work experience, the bases for group formation among women are weak. The socialization of women differs from that of men in all societies: whatever form it takes, it results most often in low feelings of political efficacy in contemporary situations.[2] Standard explanations thus, may help account for the relatively low levels of female participation in political activity, especially interest group formation and office holding.

The outlook of the discipline studying politics and existing models of politicization partially explain the roles women play in politics. However, many

---

[2]In societies with high degrees of social stratification, sex is just one among many bases of differentiation that the society imposes on its members. In Albert's words "The inferiority of women as women is only a special case of the general form of inferiority" (1971:188).

Throughout this essay the point has been made that vast heterogeneity exists among women in developing countries. While the focus of the essay has been on identifying common factors which are related to women's roles and status, equal emphasis has been placed on the divertisy of conditions surrounding women. This is made most obvious when the patterns of social stratification in any specified society are scrutinized: women at each level have differing roles and status. Upper class/caste or elite women almost always are more politically active than women of lower echelons. Not enough systematic cross-cultural work has been done to make further comparisons.

academics and activists find these explanations unsatisfactory. Women are increasingly drawn into political action in the 1970's; analysts want to predict the causes and consequences of the changes women are experiencing. Two main approaches to predicting the conditions under which women enter politics appear in the literature. Ward (1963) put forward one approach more than a decade ago. Citing variations among the Southeast Asian countries to levels of women's participation, she linked these variations to characteristics of the sociopolitical cultures. Ward's emphasis was on accounting for differences, her paradigm remained the only systematic one until recently. Recent analyses acknowledge the small variations that Ward observed in levels and kinds of participation but start with the observation that women are not active in the leadership of any country. This second group of inquirers ask what causes the almost universal lack of participation in politics among women and how the old patterns have begun to erode in the last few years.

Factors enhancing women's political participation. Ward launches her analysis of *Women in the New Asia* by considering the aspects of social change having greatest impact on women—modern medical measures, new communications networks, urbanization, modern education, and the political emancipation coupled with independence. Given the changing social environment of Asian women, Ward postulates four different forms their political participation takes. Women now hold the *franchise* in all Asian countries, often for the first time. They are eligible to run for and/or *hold office* at all levels of government. Women are encouraged to engage in *activities outside the home* in the name of "modernization.' Finally, they have differing levels of *political awareness*, stemming from membership in political organizations, exposure to modern communications, participation in new residential patterns, as well as different personal backgrounds. Ward points out important differences among these forms of participation. Exercising the franchise is a form of personal concern while holding office entails exercising power over others. Freedom to engage in activities outside the home (however much they are extensions of domestic concerns) differs from developing a political awareness of how to achieve goals. Asian women exhibit all forms of participation, in varying combinations.

Ward then turns to a discussion of what accounts for the forms of participation women take. She sets up three conditions which enhance all four kinds of involvement. An important sociological condition, according to Ward, is a non-restrictive traditional family structure and a division of labor between men and women. She finds "that the relative statuses of men and women are

41

more likely to be equal and their respective roles less rigidly demarcated in societies which emphasized radial rather than unilineal methods of reclining kinship" (92). Historically, women's participation in prolonged anti-colonial or other political struggles enhances participation because it gives women direct exposure to and experience in the political arena. Finally, Ward suggests that a religious system which can accomodate at least a fair degree of social change also encourages women's participation in politics. Although "traditional religious attitudes will reflect and support traditional social practices and will probably be rather slow to change, the degree and effectiveness of their conservative influence differ considerably with differences in dogma and ecclesiastical organization" (67). Ward finds only Islam "inevitably resistant to change in general, and change in the position of women in particular" (67). Her emphasis on the causes of variation ends on an optimistic note: the changing Asian cultural environment seemed to be leading to increasing political participation for women in the early 1960's.

Constraints on women's participation. Scholars and activities writing in the 1970s are less sure than Ward was that increased modernization automatically has positive consequences for women's entrance into politics. This more recent group of analysts, represented in collections like those of Pescatello (1972), Jaquette (1974), Raphael (1975), Leavitt (1975), and Iglitzin and Ross (1976), are still concerned with the factors enhancing women's participation. But they are uniformally less sanguine about the prospects for far-reaching changes in women's role in politics. Their concern instead is with the basic causes for lack of participation. The causes they cite fall into several groups.[3]

(1) While increased levels of education and greater involvement in professional occupations are correlated with higher levels of political participation, women's contribution to professional and political life is an extrapolation of women's maternal role to the public arena. Chaney (1972), in a comparison of Peruvian and Chilean women in politics, argues strongly that in spite of the differences between the "progressive" political climate of Chile and the more "traditional" one of Peru, women stick to extensions of the domestic maternal role in public affairs. This tendency means that

---

[3]I quote these studies at length to fully convey to readers the nature of the arguments.

42

All the barriers against the successful aspiration of women to high political office—old regimes resistant to new political aspirants of either sex, the retun to 'business as usual' after extraordinary events, the resumption of passive attitudes when the novelty of suffrage wears off, the reluctance of political parties to push women candidates—are facts which 'explain' women's disadvantaged position only in a limited way; these facts themselves require further explanation. Other obvious, straight-forward facts already have been discussed, among them women's much greater involvement in bearing and rearing children, women's concentration in the 'wrong' professions for political recruitment, or very simply the fact (of which many women party leaders are aware) that cultural and social prejudices have prevented women from forming a sufficiently large pool of capable potential political leaders to whom responsible positions might be offered.

Probably no ultimate explanations are possible, but it would seem that the questions of political leadership and the policy-making process in general (as distinct from the less controversial act of voting which often is not very important in a society) are crucial for women because it is *here* that they have made the least headway in the contemporary world. Indeed, if we are to believe what the statistics seem to tell us about women's political leadership, the situation actually has deteriorated from an emotionally induced 'high' immediately after World War II. At best, there is a stage of stagnation; if women are not going backward, they certainly are not advancing . . .

As an intermediate explanation we may logically turn first to all those prevailing images of women existing in the minds of men and women in many cultures, but perhaps less changing in the Latin American *ambiente* than in any other society. Many observers have noted the dominant, aggressive masculine and the submissive female images which most Latin American societies regard as 'ideal' because in the Latin view they are ordained by sacred natural law and confirmed by four centuries of history and convention. Sex-related differentiation between men and women is nowhere more starkly defined than in the sphere of politics, not only in Latin America, but everywhere. In Duverger's view, the hostility to political activity for women is based on the same kind of primitive mentality that sees war as a 'sport for men.' There is a similar tendency, he says, to regard the club, the forum, debates,

43

parliament and political life in general as 'typically masculine activities' (125-126).

(2)   The idea of spillover—that professional advancement for women will spillover into political influence—is not accurate because change in political systems is segmentary not systemic. Lapidus (1974) critiques modernization theories by using the example of sex roles in the Soviet Union. She says:

> The whole process of modernization, then, vastly intensifies the social strain experienced by women by confronting them with contradictory imperatives. The ideology of modernity, with its emphasis on freedom, equality and achievement as supreme and universal norms, and on competitive, instrumental personality traits, collides with pervasive cultural norms, supported by social realities, which transmit conflicting images of ideal feminine roles and attributes.

These contrasting views of the consequences of modernization for women's roles reflect divergent concerns as well as different values in appraising the outcomes of long-term social change. But they reflect, as well, more basic conceptual problems which broadly underly the study of modernization (245).

In surveying the changing roles of Soviet women since 1917, we find that a partial assimilation to male roles has occurred in the economy and policy. Levels of female participation in both the industrial labor force and in the political system have increased enormously. If women have been successfully mobilized for these purposes, they have not, however, achieved substantial equality in roles which involve managerial or political authority. Nor have they been freed from primary responsibility for family affairs, where no significant redefinition of male and female roles has occurred. Evolutionary models of development are inadequate to describe the complex pattern of social change.

Nor are systemic models of great utility in analyzing Soviet development patterns. Economic, political, and family roles have changed in different ways in response to different forces. The period of greatest political mobilization was one in which relatively little change occurred in economic roles, while the entry of women into the industrial labor force on a large scale has been compatible with sharply variant policies

44

toward the family. Neither have changes in economic organization been decisive for the broader patterning of women's roles. The economic independence of women, however, far-reaching its consequences in other respects, has not dramatically transformed the structure of status and authority in economic and political life nor has it radically altered cultural definitions of male and female roles outside the work arena. Thus, the very success of Leninism as a strategy for politically forced development calls into question Marxian models of social change which stress its evolutionary and systemic character. The Soviet experience suggests that the character of the development process, rather than the fact of development per se, is decisive in shaping women's roles. Cultural norms and political choices and capabilities become more significant than socioeconomic determinants. Both the desire and the capability to alter existing societal arrangements become central.

Precisely because the character, goals, and capabilities of the political system are of such importance, the process of change is complex. In the short run, at least, the timing, sequence, and direction of change in different sectors may take different forms. The Soviet pattern illuminates the degree to which societies are segmentary rather than systematic, and suggests the variety of amalgams which may emerge (254).

(3)   A country's cultural environment, its definition of female and male spheres, remains the most important factor affecting women's participation in politica. While the cultural milieu is obviously subject to change, modifying it is a more long term, complex, and difficult task than most political activists assume. Jancor (1974) develops a model for explaining women's position in politics. Although her research is based on women under Communism, the models' applicability is much wider.

The model involves four sets of factors: (1) The environment denotes the economic level of development, the philosophic orientation and the political system of the country or countries under consideration. (b) Leadership guidance involves both the prescribing and promotional functions of the leadership in effecting social change. The prescribing function refers to explicit legislation, party resolutions, and administrative regulations which have as their aim the clarification of social objectives and the justification of the measures taken to reach them.

45

The promotional function concerns the leadership's control and exploitation of mass media and other communications mechanisms to induce public concensus noncoercively as regards the validity of the social objectives currently pursued. (c) The female self-concept refers to the internalization by women of various role options, such as the traditional family-childbearing role, the professional role, the political role. (d) The status of women is seen as the product of the interaction of the four variables . . . .

The model hypothesizes that leadership guidance, the female self-concept and the female status position operate within the framework of the economic, philosophic and political structures of the communist system. The inner part of the circle may be considered the area of political activity, as opposed to the political environment, the operative organization of politics, which determines the rules of political activity. The model indicates that leadership guidance has a direct influence on the female status position (signified by the solid line) and an indirect influence on her self-concept (signified by the dotted line). The interaction between the female self-concept and her status position is also direct, as achievement of any kind brings about a positive redefinition of self, at least to some degree. Both the female self-concept and the female status position react back on the content of leadership guidance; the former again indirectly, the latter, directly, as status is an indicator of participation in the ruling elite. The environment thus forms the basic frame of reference within which political activity takes place, while the interchange between the three factors within the circle feeds back information to modify the environment (219-220).

Application of the model to the Communist experience leads Jancor to conclude:

1. Leadership capabilities in a coercive type of modernizing process are limited. Governments have to select priorities. These must involve economic development, social transformation to the extent necessary to promote this development, and the maintenance of power to affect additional increases in leadership capabilities. To realize these objectives, communist ruling groups had to break up the traditional family structures and mobilize women into the work world, but needed to give little attention to revolutionizing the female status.

46

2. The more traditional a society, the greater the role leadership guidance can play in its social and economic transformation. The only communist leadership which evidently believed a radical approach to the question of women was essential to the modernization process was the Chinese. It was no accident that the communes were aimed at the complete destruction of the traditional Confucian family. The Soviet attack on the Muslim family in Central Asia comes somewhat under this category as well. In Western Russia and Eastern Europe, where the family had already evolved into the conjugal limited kinship form, strong government direction was unnecessary. Hence, the leaderships in these countries could respond to the economic and political demands of modernization without mounting an all-out assault on traditional values. Such a policy reinforced their power position by securing a certain measure of male popular support.

3. Caught between this interaction between the environment and leadership capability, the behavior of women under communism has tended to be determined by habit and acquiescence to established cultural patterns. As a consequence, they have been unable to exercise

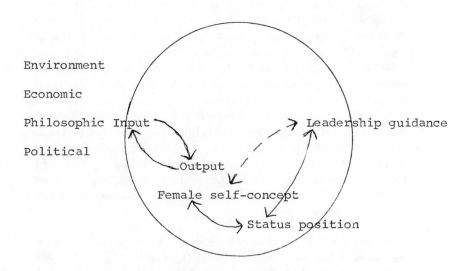

Interaction model of possible factors involved in women's status position in communist systems (Jancar 1974:220).

any real power. Groups which rise to elite status expect to derive some advantage from their new position. The evidence suggests that women in the communist systems as yet see little advantage to be gained by a change in status which might replace their traditional role (238-239).

(4)   An active women's political organization is critical to insure a permanent place for women in politics. The amalgam of individuals, small groups and organizations collectively called the women's movement in the United States is creating such an organization (McWilliams 1974). The political strength of women in Guinea (Dobert 1970; Van Allen 1974b) and in Cuba (Kaufman 1972) is buttressed by independent women's organizations. Chaney's analysis of the failure of the Allende regime to mobilize women attributes it in part to the lack of organization among women (Chaney 1974). She says

> This situation leads us to ask what is holding women back. Before we can answer this question with any certainty, we may need to devise entirely new frameworks and theoretical concepts to deal with the data of women's behavior. Women in most societies do not, for example, fit any of the current models through which political scientists attempt to analyze the phenomena of politics. They are not an elite; they do not, as a group, seek power; they do not form coalitions to bargain with other power contenders. Women are so unorganized and ill-defined as a group and command so few political resources that to regard them as forming an interest group in the same sense as industrial laborers, the military or landowners would be misleading. Nor does a simple economic/class explanation of women's inferior position appear adequate. The three Marxist women analysts mentioned above no longer accept such a thesis, nor expect (as the men appear to believe) that women will be available for full political and intellectual participation in the revolution as soon as they can be drawn into socially productive work. They all agree that doing productive work outside the home is the precondition for changing women's status, but they insist that obstacles in the sociocultural superstructure must be directly attacked if women are to be free.
>
> Many current attempts at explanation of women's inferior status are based upon sociological concepts; they prove equally unsatisfactory because they imply that all women are uniformly oppressed. Countries vary dramatically on the ranges of options they offer women,

48

and even within countries, regions, and cities, there are great gaps between the privileged and the poor. Women as women therefore cannot be classed as marginals; neither are they outcastes or second-class citizens, although substantial numbers of women may form part of all these groups in a given country (274-275).

An alternate explanation which may be more valid because it accounts more completely for the inferiority of women in every caste and class is the fact that for centuries only one approved role was open to women: motherhood. Whatever her social position, the woman's major validation lay in producing children. The woman who married and failed to achieve motherhood was pitied; the woman who did not marry despised. Because she broke the link in the generations, in many societies the single woman's life was counted a waste, and her very existence became a tragic burden to herself and to her family.

One can readily comprehend why motherhood was woman's only possible option in the early centuries of humankind's existence. Women had little choice but to passively receive children up to nature's biological limit (276).

The tasks of motherhood were in their nature hidden, unspectacular, unchanging, unconnected with any power nexus. If all women were destined for motherhood, then no special distinction was possible to women except to become outstanding mothers or to seek a surrogate motherhood in a womanly profession.

As a consequence, when the woman begins to move out to the larger society, the boundaries and style of her participation are profoundly influenced by her classic role as mother and preserver of the race. Most women go into fields analogous to the tasks they perform in the home, preeminently education and welfare of women and children. But women do not improve their inferior position very much by turning professional. Feminine fields are neither prestigious nor powerful because they are associated with the hidden, unspectacular tasks of birth and nurture, tasks which males never have deemed important.

Nothing is more natural than that women's first ventures into public life should have been put in the framework of their traditional vocation

49

as wives and mothers and should emphasize moral values. What is remarkable is that the horizons of influential women so often still are confined exclusively to these feminine interests (277).

(5)   Individual reaction to changing conceptions of women's roles also must occur for women to become politically active. How individuals become aware subjectively of their objective situation and begin to evaluate that situation is difficult to understand. Boals (1974) analyzes the determinants of women's political participation from the level of the individual psyche. Her model focuses on the interaction between culturally new and/or dominant, and culturally traditional and/or oppressed groups within a society. It outlines six stages of consciousness which individuals (and groups) may arrive at as they attempt to structure their lives while in the midst of social and cultural change. At the *traditional*, or pre-change level, an individual unquestioningly accepts the desirability of the status quo, for he or she perceives no alternative. The individual at the *traditionalist* stage however, has been confronted with alternative and often contradictory options and explanations. He or she continues to reaffirm the traditional world-view while also beginning to question the established order. Some individuals (*assimilationists*) attempt to overcome the gap between cultures by wholly identifying with the new and disassociating themselves from the traditional. The *reformist* solution is to take certain aspects of the "modern" culture and ground them in the traditional, while the *revolutionary* totally discredits the dominant culture while remythologizing the traditional in its place. These last four stages are only partial solutions for resolving the conflict between two opposing beliefs. In order to reach the final or *modernist* stage, it is necessary to become free of both cultures. Only then, Boals says, is there sufficient autonomy to create "new combinations of personality traits, lifestyles, and ways of being" without being constrained by any one cultural model.

Women's participation in politics, other than as voters, tends to be low. It is subject to variation cross-nationally and to change at the instigation of governments and/or women's organizations. While occasionally one finds women in high office, the mass of women in that country do not pursue politics as actively as men. But nowhere do women yet have the political clout to match their emergent educational and economic strength. The reasons for this gap rest with the images and ideologies societies have of women's place, and images and ideologies are more resistant to change than university enrollment figures or percentages of women in the professions.

CHAPTER VIII

IDEOLOGY AND CONTROL: WOMEN'S POSITION IN TRADITIONAL SOCIETIES

Shirley Lindenbaum

Ideology is a significant factor in sustaining cultural beliefs about the spheres and roles for women. Ideology and control over women are the subject of the Lindenbaum chapter included in this monograph. Lindenbaum stresses that one must look beyond the overt characteristics of any belief system to how that belief system reflects the realities of social life.

There have been three moments of reappraisal in recent European history concerning the relationship of women to men—the Elizabethan period, the Victorian era and the present. Each moment occurs at a time of technological and demographic change which results in a shake-up and redefinition of the work force. The Elizabethan period witnessed the emergence of a new commercial society and a break with medieval conventions and Roman Catholicism, which led to the formation of new opinions on women, marriage, and the home. Puritanism advocated the doctrine of personal responsibility, a female monarch was on the throne, and the topic of the relative worth of male and female was a matter for review. The independent behavior of Elizabethan women was not without its critics, as a proclamation issued in 1548 indicates. It forbade women "to meet together to babble and talk" and ordered men "to keep their wives in their houses" (Oakley 1972:10). Changes accompanying the Industrial Revolution again disrupted the relative symmetry in the status of women and men, led to expressions of female dissatisfaction and to the Victorian debates over sex differences. The first "woman's movement" is said to have found expression in the 1830's, when rural families had migrated to urban settings, and the value of the family as a work group was transformed. Men were now employed in jobs away from home, and their wives and children could no longer participate in the joint labor venture, becoming instead economic dependents and in many cases, liabilities. Poor families, unable to afford the luxury of such a conversion of their personnel, were forced to send their women and children to undesirable work in factories, mines or domestic service (Oakley 1972, Blake 1974). All women had suffered a loss in socially valued economic input.

Examples from our own culture are illuminating in several ways. They indicate, in the first place, that the demand for labor varies, and that if the demand is great enough, the widest social spectrum will be called to join the labor force. When the demand shrinks, however, particular categories of labor are excluded. Our recent history, then, presents a picture of women workers shuttling in and out of the public economic arena—largely dispensed with during the Industrial Revolution, for instance, but called out again during two World Wars (Troy 1972). It is significant that it is in countries chronically short of workers in the most recent years—France and Sweden—that there has been a lively examination of those aspects of women's position which might impede their more extensive participation in the work force (Blake 1974). It may be no coincidence, then, that the Equal Rights Amendment in the United States appears to be foundering at a time of economic decline, when the definition of approved workers is being more narrowly defined. Labor unions are presently facing such sticky problems as the relative priorities of length of service or the civil rights of minorities, while illegal aliens whose labor contribution was condoned in the booming sixties are now being identified so that they may be pruned from the work force. The lesson is clear—loss of economic contribution leads to social discrimination.

Examples taken from our own society reveal also something of the relationship between ideology and control, between a set of shared ideas and the manipulation of components of the population. The sturdy, practical women of pre-industrial times, who carried her share of the family's earnings, was replaced by the romantic, inhibited, swooning Victorian female, corseted in her clothing and cloistered in the home (Blake 1974). We should be alert then, whenever we come across a definition of female and male roles inflected with a heavy ideological or moral component. The biological or sexual difference in female and male performance is invariable; variations on the theme are cultural, or a matter of gender (Oakley 1972). The most recent public figure to attempt to confuse the two categories is former Senator Sam Ervin who, descending from the Blue Ridge Mountains to speak against the Equal Rights amendment, noted that ... "You cannot put equal responsibility on men for being mother to children" (New York Times, March 20, 1975). This is the same fudging of biology and culture used until recently to justify the nonemployment of young women as

52

Senatorial pages—that the Senate Building was not equipped with toilets for women.

Ideological transitions can be abrupt. In July, 1944, women made up 34.7% of the American labor force; by November, 1946, their numbers had dropped to 18.9%. While the war lasted, women were encouraged as United States citizens and partners in the United Nations to help in the struggle against fascism, which was presented as an enslaver of peoples and a foe of the progress of women (Trey 1972). At war's end, however, women were again counselled by former employers and by speakers at college graduation that their proper place was in the home, and their only vocation, motherhood (Trey 1972).

Just as European and American women shift in and out of a variety of economic occupations, women in other cultures are found performing diverse economic roles of differing social worth. A survey of 185 societies records certain activities as almost invariably performed by men (Murdock and Provost 1972). Yet in some societies, these "masculine activities" may also be carried out by women, such as woodwork (by Pawnee women), the manufacture of musical instruments (Tuareg women), and boatbuilding (Hidatsa females). Mbuti Pygmy women are found trapping small animals, and women among the Fur collect iron ore (Murdock and Provist 1973). Despite such examples of the capacity of women to carry out tasks allotted by most societies to men, there is also general agreement that there are a number of constants to the division of labor by sex (Hammond and Jablow 1973). Women are found, on the whole, doing those things which are compatible with the nursing and care of children. Since she not only feeds but transports the suckling child, a woman's work is not compatible with danger, mobility, or travelling long distances. Her subsistence activities tend to be performed not far from home, they are not dangerous, and can be frequently interrupted and resumed. This rules out warfare, hunting, herding of large animals and long distance trade, which are generally masculine activities. Since physical strength has little to do with the allocation of tasks, women are frequently found to be the water-carriers and collectors of firewood. Some New Guinea Highland women return from the garden at day's end with a load of firewood balanced on top of the head, a string bag of sweet potatoes supported by a headband, and another headband supporting the infant's carrying bag—a total headweight of about 50-60 pounds, or at least half the mother's body weight.

In general, then, while hunting, herding of large animals, and plow agriculture (which demands the monitoring of large animals) brings forth a

53

predominantly male labor force, most subsistence activities in gathering and horticultural (hoe agriculture) societies are performed by females. While it is true that in societies where women contribute little to subsistence production, their status is uniformly low (Sanday 1973), yet it is not the case that in those societies where women's labor contributes most to subsistence, that their social status is greater than that of men.

This suggests that women's contribution to the economy should be looked at more closely. It is often noted that woman's work is domestic and private, in contrast to the public and social pre-occupations of men. Moreover, in performing the ascribed tasks allotted to them as sisters, wives or mothers, women do not have access to the prestige and status flowing from public, male achievements (Rosaldo 1974). The domestic/public dichotomy is clearly illustrated, for example, by looking at the participation of women and men in stone-age trade in New Guinea before it was modified by colonial intrusion. Men are shown to have dominated the production, transfer, and consumption of trade goods. Men made the stone axes, collected the best pigments and oils, birds and animals, furs and feathers, and these were the items of trade. Luxury crops, like pandanus nuts, were men's crops, and were traded, while the main product of women's labor, staple root crops and green vegetables, were not included as exchange items. If a woman received valuables, such as shell ornaments, she did so as a custodian only. Thus, while women in New Guinea contribute most to subsistence food production, the prestige occupations, luxury crops, and public esteem are exclusively male.

This marked feature of economic life among neolithic peoples is very like the differential pattern of participation in the economy remarked upon by observers of capitalist societies—that women's labor is unpaid, outside of trade and the marketplace, and is pre-capitalist in a very real sense (Benston 1989). Commodities, it is noted, have both use-value and exchange-value, but women's work—since it focuses on the things produced in the home for home consumption—has use but not exchange-value.

It is sometimes overlooked that women themselves are items of trade, components of the market transactions among groups of men. As commodities, they too appear to embody both kinds of value. In Bangladesh, for instance, at the time of marriage, the two kinds of value are experienced in rapid succession. As she approaches marriage age, a young woman's value as a productive asset (her use-value) is de-emphasized. Through mounting cultural emphases, which

54

have little to do with biological need, she is progressively turned into a symbol of luxury (her exchange-value). Her public visibility is made scarce, while the economic burdens of keeping her in feminine attire increase. The greater the capacity of her family to distance her from any suggestion of productive activity, the greater her value as a symbol of luxury. Young marriageable girls are often prompted to exhibit their needlework—embroidered pillow cases with poetic messages suggesting the development of these refined skills in idle hours. The rewards of this 'image-management' accrue to her family in the social elevation of a prestigious marriage alliance.

The young bride, newly severed from a household where she has been treated as a most precious object, makes a sometimes bumpy transition to the house of her husband, where she becomes a servant to the older generation, works hard and speaks little. Her productive value as a worker in her husband's family is high, but her value as a luxury good is very low. The cultural transition for the bride is thus abrupt, a stress sometimes resulting in manifestations of autistic behavior. (To compare the suicide rate of Chinese brides at a similar moment, see Yang 1965). From a luxury object, she is now abruptly redefined as a capital asset, and her gradual regaining of status depends on the ability to give birth to sons, and the consequent accumulation of the sumbolic values surrounding motherhood (Lindenbaum 1975).

We are faced with the fact that gender is and may have been a basic distinction and a basis for ranking in the social organization of all societies. Since women at first marriage are generally younger than their husbands, age adds to sex in the allocation of status (Rosenblatt & Cunningham in press). Although women may acquire influence and power, men everywhere retain authority (Friedl 1967, Rosaldo 1974). The biological distinction between the sexes has everywhere provided the basis for an asymmetrical system of classification—in some societies more elaborate than in others.

In Bangladesh, again, a number of dichotomies, both symbolic and real, support a marked distinction between the sexes, most visible in the seclusion of women. The preference for males over females is coded into a variety of dual messages. Men are associated with the right, favored, pure side of things, women with the left and all the antonyms of the above. The pulse of males, it is believed, registers in the right wrist, of females in the left, and village practitioners invariably examine patients in this way. Amulets worn to deflect illness caused by evil influences, are tied to the right arm of males, to the left of females. The entrance to public places, such as the tombs of Muslim saints or the display of Hindu images, reserves entrance for men by the right, women by the left. Islam underlines the idea of preference in the right/left dichotomy. Angels, it is believed, dwell on the right shoulder recording good deeds in preparation for the Day of Judgment. On the left side, devils record all misdeeds. The left side is more than the devil's location—it is associated with the concept of pollution. The left hand should be reserved for cleansing the body of impurities, and must never be used to convey food to the mouth, to rinse the mouth with water before daily prayers, or to offer gifts.

Related to these dual categories is the revealing social arithmetic that two women together equal the value of one man. In Muslim inheritance, for example, one brother's share equals that of two sisters, while as legal witnesses, it is said, "If there are not two men, then one man and two women." The symbolic shorthand of these right-left, two-one categorizations sets apart and reinforces the roles of men and women in a hierarchical way. It is a cultural code for the political and social realities of Bangali life (Lindenbaum 1968).

Many societies do not demonstrate so refined a distinction in relations between the sexes. Indeed, in some societies, it appears that the battle between the sexes is still being waged. This brings us to the matter of ideological control.

The idea that some individuals or groups are a danger to others, because of their powers of pollution, is a widespread concept. It is used to construct the major hierarchical arrangements of Hindu society, whereby individuals belonging to lower castes in the social order are believed to pollute those in the ranks above. Brahmans, who occupy the top position, may be polluted by all categories below them, while castes at the bottom are believed to pollute the rest of society, and thereby suffer an accumulation of economic and social discriminations. More universally, the concept of pollution is used to distance and separate the social and political arrangements of women and men.

It is an idea which emerges quite early in human social evaluation, and it flourishes in the horticultural societies of New Guinea. Among the Fore of the Eastern Highlands of New Guinea, for instance, women are the acknowledged locus of two kinds of resource, fertility and labor, and the attempt to control these two variables in one person gives rise to the tangled field of sexual politics. Women's sexuality is the dangerous "wild" which men must bring under control. Much of the initiation for young men involves males playing on sacred flutes (symbolic penises, said to have been captured from women by trickery) and the periodic letting of blood from the nose in rituals of imitative menstruation. The discarded blood is said to be a freezing of accumulated female contamination acquired by contact with women. Both sexes are secluded during their periodic bleeding, but while women are excluded, men withdraw voluntarily, and only the latter is associated with a gain in status. The entire ritual complex in New Guinea allows men to state their all-round social and biological superiority in a sacred context.

By pretending to male menstruation, New Guinea males are carving out a political domain by taking public responsibility for important aspects of reproduction and human survival. Fore men make public speeches of the need to plant new gardens and inseminate their wives. It is also the Fore husband, rather than his wife, who observes the food taboos and behavioral restraints in order to steer the child safely through the pregnancy and post-partum period. There is an orchestrated sense of the universe under male constraint.

Yet there is one significant area over which men claim no control—the birth of deformed infants. This is said to be the sole responsibility of women, and the husband and all the men of the community treat it as a great pollution. They punish the mother by killing one of her pigs, then quit the area of contamination to gather at the water's edge in the forest, where they purify themselves with blood-letting, and eat fortifying medicines. They return that evening to the community of shamed wives. Older women express their resentment by waiting in ambush to beat the men's legs with stinging nettles, a small ritual of rebellion. The men thus maintain a kind of quality control over the human population. They dramatize their role as arbiters, indicating that they consider this less-than-human thing brought forth by women to be a kind of sexual insurrection. The polluting female has been disciplined by a ceremony of social degradation (Lindenbaum in press).

Where we find a society in which men, in contrast, are believed to pollute women, we should then be alert to indications of a more symmetrical political order. On the New Guinea island of Wegeo, for instance, a society organized by matrilineal kinship reckoning, men are reported to have power to pollute women. Here we find that husband and wife are economically dependent on one another, adultery by both sexes is common, and after the birth of children neither husband nor wife can initiate divorce. Wogeo women appear to take unusual ritual levities, since part of a young girl's coming-of-age celebration includes a mock version of the initiation rite for pubescent youths, something they are supposed to know nothing about. This is not treated altogether lightly by the men, who storm the women's ritual ground and drive them away with sticks and stones (Hogbin 1970). It has been suggested that cross-sex violence during courtship, tests of male/female strength in playful wrestling matches, and similar evidence of the domestic war of the sexes, is characteristic of societies with relative freedom concerning choice of spouse (Rosenblatt 1972). It should be noted at this point, that despite rules of matrilineal kinship among the Wogeo, and the fact that women in that society enjoy a higher status than is customary in New Guinea, they do not occupy prior place. Women "exert" authority only in the domestic circle, and in the wider political sphere are powerless (Hogbin 1970:86). Ideas about pollution, honor, and shame (Schneider 1971) and other moral inflections on biological status then, are the means by which men in a number of societies exert control over the women they consider their legal property—their wives, sisters or daughters. The effect is achieved by collapsing the two categories of biology and culture, by presenting physiological attributes in moral form, by thinking about women as commodities (she menstruates = she is dirty; she is not a virgin = she is worthless).

Some societies use more forceful ideas to comment on the appropriate or inappropriate activities of women. In some instances, women are accused of witchcraft, the accusation relating to the women's economic ventures. In postcolonial times, Nupe women of Northern Nigeria have become extensive traders, acquiring considerable income. Nupe men view these societies of female traders as societies of witches. Nadel, who lived among Nupe in the mid 1930's, also noted an additional association between female trade and prostitution. It has been observed, however, that in Yoruba society, virtually all women are traders, suggesting that the cause for the charge of immorality there goes beyond the deviant sexual behavior of a small proportion of women in each society (Mintz 1971).

It would seem that, just as the fusion of sex and moral evaluation provides the ideology of political control, the husbands of economically powerful women again express their diminished position with arguments of moral-biology. A similar version of the contest arose recently in Bangladesh (then East Pakistan) concerning an unusual economic venture, the formation of a small rural women's consumer co-operative. The co-operative appears to have had some initial success, the women gaining a license to import coconut oil from Ceylon. The full story of the co-operative's demise is somewhat unclear, but one major criticism was voiced by the male kin of co-operative members who felt that female economic autonomy was leading to immoral behavior. The women were accused of spending their earnings riding into town by rickshaw, wearing lipstick, and of visiting movies. The potential economic domination of the market by women in both the Bangali and Nupe cases is viewed as contrary behavior, a kind of sexual deviance. The problem of women achieving some kind of independence without giving up the traditional relationship between women and men is, as Pauline Kael notes (New Yorker, January 13, 1975), the problem confronted by the new-style angry woman movies like 'Alice Doesn't Live Here Any More.' As the myths of the Fore of New Guines indicate, stories about men stealing the sacred flutes from women by male trickery and violence, are myths about the subjugation of women. They are also embryonic statements in the history of the battle of men to control women's bodies, probably among the first power plays in human evolution, a point to be returned to again.

The entire topic of the relationship of ideology to behavior is a complex one. Ideology appears to emerge where overt control or alternate institutional controls are lacking. It is a kind of public relations campaign to modify the behavior of imperfectly contained subordinate groups. Mary Douglas has argued that the dogma of ritual contamination by females may be expected where males find that their authority can be challenged, but is absent where the husband enforces discipline by ruthless force, allowing women no leverage in playing one man off against another. The literature on the polluting female would seem to confirm her point. Women as agents of social disorder are both dirty and dangerous (Douglas 1966).

Some witchcraft accusations may be directed to the same end. Epstein notes accusations of witchcraft against a new class of money-lending women in Mysore, whose successful business dealings defy the sexual hierarchy and the traditional values allowing long-term credit in patron-client relations. There is a significant absence of such accusations against men, or between castes, where ordered relations are regulated by social institutions, where the relations are highly formalized, and the rights and duties are clearly recognized by all concerned (Epstein 1959). Ideologies are called into play to bond, regulate and order contradictory relationships, or to settle disputes in the interest of the establishment, where no regulatory mechanism otherwise exists. The idea may be illustrated again if we view romantic love as a functional substitute for subsistence dependence. In effect, romantic love arises where there is an absence of a division of labor by sex great enough to produce the subsistence dependence of one sex upon the other (Coppinger and Rosenblatt 1968). As Pauline Kael comments of the new 'woman' movies, they are not just about a romance in trouble, "It's romance itself that's in trouble" (Kael 1975).

Angry, frustrated women, however, are not a phenomenon of the 1975 theatre season. There is a great deal of literature indicating that anomalous and powerless individuals in many societies may be particularly vulnerable to possession by spirits (Lewis 1971). Hausa women of Northern Nigeria, for instance, become members of a Bori cult, through which married women excluded from public life and office-holding (after a carefree, mobile childhood), experience a kind of fantasy of political power, status, and drama otherwise denied them. Since the spirit possessing the woman, and not the woman herself, is believed responsible for her behavior, women are also free to demand real rewards, concessions, and gifts from authoritarian husbands.

Similar cults occur throughout the world, in which women use this special strategy of possession to state in acceptable form things they are not free to express directly. Such cults have been reported in Ethiopia, the Muslim Sudan, Egypt, and in parts of North Africa and Arabia. A sex-linked possession syndrome occurs also with female shamans in Southeast Asia, India, China, and Japan. Women, as in Victorian times, swoon, faint, and take on some special kind of affliction to get the attention, the economic luxuries, or the manipulation over others that they are not free to ask for directly. Lewis notes that where such possession states and trances occur—and sometimes the cult groups have male membership—we are not dealing with bizarre forms of mass neurosis, but with embryonic protest movements. It is a sobering thought that Phyllis Chessler conveys then, when she argues that political forces create or define the categories of abnormality in society, noting that women, black and white and of all social classes (particularly unmarried women) comprise the largest group of psychiatrically hospitalized and 'treated' Americans (Chessler (1971).

There is one final fact of female life which remains to be discussed, women's fertility. The control of female fertility is perhaps the ultimate political instrument, one of the first political issues, and one still being fought in abortion law debates in many countries. It is not just a matter of legal control over children, but of controlling fertility outcome.

It is significant that Nupe husbands described by Nadel were troubled by more than the reversal of roles by which their wives had assumed many of the financial responsibilities considered to belong to the family head—such as finding bride price for sons as well as paying for the children's education and family feasts. They were also concerned by the fact that in order to become itinerant traders, some women had refused to burden themselves with additional children by practicing abortion and allegedly using contraceptives. In traditional pre-colonial times, men had controlled long distance trade, and local trade was reserved for sterile women or those past child-rearing (Nadel 1942:153,333). This association of witchcraft with anti-social sex and sexuality is encountered in many societies, not just among the Nupe. Witches are sometimes identified as old women past childbearing, and thus in a sense unusable reproductive material, while others are women who have borne no children and are believed to be denying human increase. (Traditional Nupe society had found an acceptable outlet for these women.) Sometimes female witches are pictured as cannibals, improper consumers of life (the Nyakusa of Tanganyika), who are themselves destroyed by society (The Hewa of New Guinea). The Abelam of New Guinea believe that witches are women who "leave their sleeping bodies and fly in the night on their evil errands, of which the most important is killing infants" (Forge 1970:268). Moreover, the power of Abelam witches is said to derive from a malicious little creature harbored in their vaginas, inactive until puberty.

In the European witch craze of the fifteenth and sixteenth centuries, persecuted female witches were said to have copulated with the devil, to have caused impotence amongst men, and to have provided contraceptive aid and performed abortions. In short, as the Malleus Maleficarum, a fifteenth century document on the procedure for conducting a witch hunt records, women were accused of obstructing the generative force in men and destroying it in women. The occurrence of female witches, of menstruating men, and the current conflict over abortion and the right-to-life suggest that power to control fertility is a fundamental male-female power issue.

Because of the linkage between female status and the correct performance of the roles of wife and mother, women are well motivated to conform to social expectations regarding reproduction. Demographers note that women respond not only to the pressure to bear the appropriate number of children, but also the desired number of each sex. Bangladesh is an agricultural society with certain labor needs. When speaking to educated Bangalis, they indicate that at the present moment the ideal family outcome would be provided by two adult sons and one married daughter, a formula curiously like the 'two-for-one' cultural code, and a family ideal similar to that in some neighboring states of India. A computer simulation for Indian conditions has shown that in order to ensure the presence of one adult son when the father reaches the age of 65, the mother must produce six and seven offspring, and that is about the average she produced both in the Indian case and in Bangladesh (Mandelbaum 1974).

Regional differences in male-female life expectancy for India and Bangladesh are somewhat more instructive as a measure of female status. Census data since 1931 suggest that overall female life expectancy is lower than that for males in India, contrary to most international experience. But within India, there are interesting regional variations. In general, females suffer a disadvantage in chances for survival in the North and North-West regions, in contrast to their position in East India and the South. Bangladesh joins the North and North-western States in having higher death rates among females, particularly in the first four years of life, a fact attributable to differences in nutrition and in health care (Lindenbaum 1975). The death rate among female children is about 50% higher than that for males in the Punjab, Uttar Pradesh, and Bangladesh, and about 20% higher in the states of Rajasthan and Gujarat. In contrast, in Assam, Jammu and Kashmir, Kerala and Karnataka, the female child has a lower death rate.

Explanations for this high regional variation in mortality among females appears also to be related to frequency of childbirth and to early childbearing, since the average number of children per woman is higher, while the median age at marriage is lower in the North and North-West, than it is in the South Indian States or in most of the East. Women in Bangladesh have an even higher fertility rate and a lower median age at marriage than in North and North-West India, producing a population growth rate of around 3% per annum.

Explanations may also be looked for in the literacy rate, which is extremely low in these North and North-Western States and in Bangladesh, affecting the access of women to public health facilities and their awareness of the importance of sanitation and food habits.

Purdah, and exaggerated concerns for the honor and safety of women, are also more prevalent in this Norty/North-Western region, as in Bangladesh, providing the ideological index we have come to expect for the low evaluation of women. We are talking here, however, about more than low social status. Women are both valued less and suffer survival disadvantages in some regions of the subcontinent, and the explanation would seem to be related to differing ecological conditions and production relations in each region (Bardhan 1974, Lindenbaum 1975).

In the Indian States where women's status and survival is higher, the predominant crop is rice paddy, drawing on the relatively intensive labor contributions of women. Women are found in these regions weeding, harvesting, and threshing paddy. By contrast, in the wheat cultivating areas of the North and North-West, the workforce is predominantly male, while women's contribution is directed toward cloistered domestic activities and to reproduction of the male work force. Rice-growing Bangladesh is an anomaly in the sense that only the poorest women contribute labor to rice production, so that the labor picture closely resembles that of the wheat-growing North. The position of women is lowest in measurable terms then, where their contribution to economic productivity is low, but their reproductive performance is high.

As an aside, it is instructive to note here, that families of high status in stratified societies such as Bangladesh and India, tend to have fewer offspring than families of lower status, since elites have access to the labor of others. It should also be noted that women in Southeast Asia have high fertility, but they participate in subsistence production, and consequently their position differs from that of women in other Islamic areas (Boserup 1970).

As a broad overview, the same kind of analysis might be made of the population needs of societies and of women's economic roles from early hunting and gathering periods until present post industrial times. Among early hunters, the motive for curbing possible births comes from the need for the mother to space infants, so she can provide both adequate food and transport, a motive which probably existed throughout the Pleistocene period. With sedentary life, this motive for child spacing diminishes, and agriculturalists, like pastoralists, have generally considered children to be an economic advantage. The demand for taxes and rents imposed by centralized rule, social stratification, and colonialism requires greater surplus production and may have further promoted population increase, placing additional demands on women in these societies. It has been suggested that the present considerations faced by parents in the modern industrial world are analogous to those in hunting and gathering societies. In the latter, it is a question of whether the child is worth the extra labor in transport and preparation of food, or the risk of depriving a sibling of milk. Parents in industrial nations face the problem of investment of time and money for the care and education now demanded by full social membership (Dumond 1975). In both, the cost of children to parents is high, the issue a personal one, and women appear to have greater autonomy in making the decision. Coercion by kin groups and state institutions seems to arise when the problem concerns stepping up achievable fecundity rather than its limitations. The Catholic Church appears to be losing this power in nations such as Brazil, where religious ideology presently conflicts with family limitation needs, telling us something further about the relationship of ideology and behavior.

Thus, the anthropological record shows that there are few biological imperatives in the allocation of work. Women are capable of performing all tasks except those which might interfere with the survival of mother and infant. Yet, sexual asymmetry is a feature of every society, and cultural elaborations serve to emphasize the difference in some societies more than in others. The relationship of women to economic production is an important one, and women confined to non-public, non-prestigious, pre-capitalist domestic labor, who are also expected to generate a largely male workforce, suffer a fatal combination of a double denial of rights in their own reproductive (biological) and productive (or cultural) performance. Where women are in a position to challenge the masculine order, ideologies of pollution and shame serve to keep them in place, while women who are not free to issue direct protest respond with illness or trance or by succumbing to states of possession. The battle to control a women's reproductive performance may be the archetypal power issue, played out in the imaginative metaphor of female witches and menstruating men, and allowing more autonomy in decision-making when the labor needs of the society are not pressing. As a last thought, since so few sexual differences in role performance seem inevitable, it may be that there are more adaptive solutions to the division of labor than that based on sex.

CHAPTER IX

THE ADVERSE IMPACT OF DEVELOPMENT

Irene Tinker

The development policies pursued by both national governments and foreign donors and agencies often have an adverse impact on women (Tinker 1976). The mechanization of agriculture, the introduction of cash crops and instructions in their cultivation, the expansion of local trade, the creation of factories in place of cottage industries, urbanization and the increasing predominance of wage labor, may all cut into the very areas of the economy where women have made the most significant contributions. Undercutting their economic base causes dislocations in other social values. The ramifications of development policies on women are the subject of the Tinker chapter included in this monograph. Prepared for presentation at a seminar held prior to the International Women's Year Conference in June, 1975, this essay stresses many of the issues debated in the Mexico City meeting.

During much of the last quarter century development has been viewed as the panacea for all the ills of the former colonial countries: pour money into a country to create an infrastructure and the economy will take off. Rostow's primer on *The Stages of Economic Growth: A Non-Communist Manifesto* (1960) is appropriately subtitled for it suggests the assumed inevitable improvement. Development specialists are increasingly aware that theories of development based on capital intensive projects may have increased the overall GNP, but at the expense of the poorest forty percent of the population. Even that estimate is based upon selective statistics which ignore whole sectors of the economy: the informal or tertiary sector, exchange labor, and the large amount of agricultural labor and food processing done within the family context. A closer look at real economic activity would also show that a majority of women are playing more restrictive economic roles today than in the pre-developed economy: women are losing out as development widens the gap between women's and men's earning power. The reason is that the western model of development exports a middle class image of what is appropriate for women's work, one that limits or undermines traditional occupations. As a result development adversely affects women in most developing countries.

The American women's movement itself is questioning these same middle class values. Yet we should be equally guilty of exporting stereotypes if we assumed women abroad were images of ourselves (Simmons 1974:1). For example, we see the nuclear family as confining and search out new forms of marriage. Yet several observers of Asian women argue that the nuclear family is the primary liberating force from the patriarchal dominance of the extended family (Metha 1970:203; Ward 1962:80-92). Latin American observers, on the other hand, suggest that the kin network which typifies traditional extended families there actually allowed for more equality of women because of the shared obligations and duties within the family (Pescatello 1963).

Similarly, the practice of seclusion, or purdah, is regarded by us as an extreme form of backwardness. Yet such seclusion is spreading today in parts of Africa and Asia: it is perceived as an improvement of status, an emulation of the status of the upper classes. Among the Hausa of northern Nigeria, farming is done by animist rural women, but the urban Muslim House women are reported to have refused to farm and preferred seclusion. Slave women among the Hausa also worked in the fields. With the abolition of slavery, these women sought to improve their status by refusing to farm. This may account for the continued willingness of Hausa women to maintain purdah. A recent study found that "most women interviewed claimed they preferred to be kept in seclusion on the grounds that it reduced their work load and raised their prestige" (Barkow 1972:323). The process of Sanskritization among Hindus—emulating the caste above your own—has led families who can afford it to stop their women from working in the fields so they may stay at home. In a searching study of purdah, Hanna Papanek has also observed an increase in women following the custom in Bangladesh (Papanek 1973).

Again, we in the West think of children as belonging by right to the mother. Under Islam, the children go to the man's family, a fact which expedites remarriage of the divorced woman. African children also traditionally remained

66

with the man's family. Recent legislation in Kenya absolving the man of his responsibility to care for his children is seen by most women there as oppressive (Wipper 1972:348). The changes introduced in the name of development have made it more difficult for women to function economically; at the same time, development has increased their burdens.

It seems clear, then, that we must try to evaluate the roles and status of women in each culture if we are to interpret the impact of development in each case. Before doing so, let me offer two caveats. First, development can improve the position of women. To date what has generally happened is that women have simply not been a factor in development planning so that little is known about the impact which schemes have in fact had. Evidence proves, however, that the stereotypes of women's occupations held by the foreign expert and the indigenous planner alike are at odds with reality. Stereotypes must go, and plans must be re-evaluated.

Secondly, we should remember that progress or development is a modern ideology, and that rise and fall is a more accurate description of history. Women's status has clearly fluctuated over the centuries. Evelyn Sullerot (1974:14) argues that:

> As a rule it is in the early periods of each civilization that the least difference exists between the position of men and that of women. As a civilization asserts and refines itself, the gap between the relative status of men and women widens.

She argues that this is due to the imposition of concepts of private property and the patriarchal family system on simpler societies where women had more options. Ebihara (1974) notes similar reductions of women's status in Southeast Asia. A Chinese visitor to the Khmer empire in Angkor Wat in the 13th century recorded that women held many positions in the court; yet within a century due to the influx of Chinese influence after the fall of the empire, women were reduced to being legal minors of their husbands.

The focus of the discussion today is on contemporary economics and the effort of western planners to assist development programs around the world. Thus we shall limit the presentation to existing societies and consider how development is changing them.

Subsistence Agriculture

In subsistence economics every family member has traditionally been assigned roles which are essential for the survival ot the unit. Assigned jobs were sex specific, but they are not always the same jobs from culture to culture. This is true in nomadic societies and in hunting and gathering societies, as well as in the early farming societies. Men and women, girls and boys, young and old, all play important roles and there is much evidence today to indicate that family units limited the number of family members to the availability of resources. Thus many societies practiced infanticide, while other societies pushed out members no longer useful, whether they were old people as with the Eskimos, or landless people as with some of the Pacific Islanders.

In subsistence economies where there is land pressure, slash and burn is the typical agricultural style. While the men clear the land, women generally do the farming. Ester Boserup, in her landmark book *Women's Role in Economic Development*, shows that as land pressure increases draft animals are brought in to increase productivity; at that point men become more involved in the farming. As land pressure increases, intensive agricultural practices replace the more extensive plow system. This is as true in traditional wet-rice systems as in the recent green revolution. Thus, while in Africa women work more hours in the fields than men, men do most of the work in Latin America and in West Asia; in Southeast Asia a balance is reached. Statistics gathered by the Economic Commission of Africa show women as agricultural laborers in Africa to vary by country and religion, but generally to constitute between 50% and 70% of the agricultural labor force. Female hours worked as a percent of male hours at 150% and goes to an amazing 450% in parts of Uganda.

Women who were farmers had rights to land. Under tribal custom these were user rights; but European colonials felt uncomfortable with customary land tenure rights and often converted land to private ownership without any understanding of the local traditions. They, like the Chinese in Southeast Asia, failed to recognize women's rights to land and so vested ownership in men. As a result, women were left with customary rights to work on land which belongs to her lineage or to that of her husband's; she has no ownership rights even where inheritance was through the female line. Inheritance of land and the obligations of succoring children in many places go together. Where the women's clan inherits the land and the wife works both on her brother's and husband's plots, she is likely to work harder on her brother's crops because it is her brother who is responsible for her children. Indeed, among the Ashanti in Ghana, wives live more often with their matrilineal kingroup than with their husband (Fortes 1958:270).

The colonial governments also introduced cash crops, especially in Africa. Even though women did the greater part of farming there, cash crops were considered a man's work. Thus men had access to income while women remained in the subsistence economy. This lack of available money and loss of control over land meant that women had little incentive to improve even land crops, a fact which helps account for the low productivity of farms in Africa. Today women still run the farms, often alone as their husbands migrate to jobs in towns or mines. Government efforts to introduce cooperatives in Kenya fell afoul of this fact; the cooperatives required the man to be the member. In Tanzania there is no sexual barrier for membership in the Ujamaa villages. All laborers are paid according to their work. Some observers assert that women are the most ardent supporters of socialist rural policies in many areas of Tanzania.

Developers incredibly continue to ignore the fact that women farm in Africa. It was reported that as recently as 1974 the government of Liberia brought in Taiwanese experts to improve rice growing in that country, and paid local men three days wages to learn the improved techniques. Of course, it is the women who farm. Extension services in Ethiopia typically consisted of men, so men who never farmed taught farming to men who were not farmers.

The green revolution has also had impact on women. In Indonesia the high capitalization involved in improved seeds and fertilizer pushed farmers into more efficient harvesting arrangements. Mechanized harvesting teams replaced handpickers, and the handpickers were women. A contrary finding comes from India where the costs of laborers were foregone and women put back in the field. An interesting side-effect in the Indian case is a reported increase in the age of marriage.

The economic utility of women affects marriage practices in most farming societies. In slash and burn societies where women are a valuable commodity, men must pay a bride price to the bride's father to buy her services. In West Asia where purdah is enforced, women never work in the fields. They become an expense, not an asset; therefore a dowry is sent from the bride's family along with her into the marriage to aid in her support. In India, dowry characterizes the upper classes but the lower castes pay a bride price for their working wives.

Besides farming, women in subsistence economies traditionally spun fibers and wove cloth, drew water, processed and preserved food. While women in Southeast Asia boiled palm sugar, West African women brewed beer, and women in parts of Mexico made pottery from coils of clay. Women from all of these cultures might sell their surplus food or goods in local markets. Profits belonged to the women themselves. Thus, women in many parts of the world became known for their astuteness in the market. Javanese women are supposed to be thrifty and foresighted with money while Javanese men consider themselves incapable of handling it wisely (H. Geertz 1961:123). In Nicaragua the women continue to dominate the indigenous stalls which cater to the lower classes in the same vicinity with super markets where the middle class go to be waited on by men. Women in West Africa have gone beyond local markets into transport, importing goods, and manufacturing. Ester Ocloo, a Ghanaian manufacturer, writes about this development:

> By the end of 1940 the scene in our marketplaces, especially in the big towns, began to change. Many of the locally produced goods began to disappear, giving place to foreign ones. Improved marketplaces were built in the big towns with well protected display stalls for textiles and other foreign goods. It was during this period that we had the market women dividing themselves into two main groups: the first group comprise women who sell farm produce, fish and locally manufactured products, such as clay pots, wooden spoons, beads, etc.; and the second group, who form the rich or well-to-do ones, sell textiles, shoes, cosmetics, tobacco and all sorts of imported items. (2).

In contrast, Hindu and Arab women are never seen in the markets as sellers and seldom as buyers. Thus, in the markets of West Africa, Muslim men sell leather goods from the north next to coastal women selling local produce. In Southeast Asia, the men prefer jobs in the bureaucracy while women and foreign men dominate the trading sector.

Technology has had considerable impact on these customary activities. Transport has opened new markets for goods which can compete with cheaply-made artifacts. In Mexico the greater demand for ceramic animal figures has brought increased income, but traditional coil pots are still made in preference to pots thrown on a kick wheel. Women everywhere sew clothes instead of making cloth. Piped water, grinding mills, as well as bus trips into town for amusement have eased the drudgery of rural life.

On the other hand, many traditional occupations become redundant. The circle of local markets may be bypassed by traders direct from towns, undercutting women traders in the outlying villages. The importation of coca cola ruined the local soft drink manufacture on Java just as did the importation of Australian ice cream. Both traditional enterprises had been dominated by women. Sago processing by women in Sarawak was replaced by machine processing run by Chinese. Men's enterprises also suffer with competition from national or international firms. A study of governmental policies in Zaria showed that the small informal sectors of the economy, run by men, suffered from the lack of services, particularly water, light and credit; this prevented their expansion. On the other hand, the large tobacco factory and the textile factory run by men were subsidized by governmental policy (Remy and Weeks 1973:9).

Similarly, education has been biased in favor of men around the world. In Africa today nine out of ten women are illiterate. The fact that there are only twenty per cent more literate men than women in Africa is a commentary on the elite character of the missionary education system. In Asia the figures go from 87% illiteracy of women in India to 52% in Hong Kong. Yet in that colonial city women are five times more likely to be illiterate than men. The higher the level of education, the fewer the women. In Africa some 20-30% of primary students are girls; in secondary school this falls to 10-20%. In South Asia, where only 2½% of the adult population continue in school after fourteen years, about one-fifth are women. In Latin America nearly half the students in higher education are women though the percentage of adults so educated varies from two to ten.

In traditional pursuits, the lack of education was no problem. Parents often kept girls from school feeling education merely delayed marriage. Elsewhere, girls were removed from school at the first sign of puberty. But as the modern sector invades the traditional sphere, women in the markets for example are at a disadvantage. Thus, the Economic Commission of Africa has launched an African Women's Development Task Force to upgrade the position of the rural woman by training them in skills, teaching bookkeeping, setting up credit and food cooperatives, teaching the use of labor-saving devices, and devising adult education courses which include farming as well as nutrition. Even more

71

impressive is the attempt to train the educated elite to work with the rural women for this purpose.

The lack of a modern education limits women's options even more when she migrates to the city. If she moves with her husband she may be able to continue household crafts or petty trading. But trading on a small scale takes place within an established circle of customers; too frequent moving can destroy a business. Women seamstresses have to compete with tailors who have easier access to credit and therefore can carry a wider supply of fabrics. Remy and Weeks (1973:17) studied the economic activity of women in Zaria and comment: "Without exception, the women in my sample who had been able to earn a substantial independent income had attended primary school . . . All of the women had learned to read, write, and speak some English."

While the married woman finds her economic independence severely limited in towns, she at least has a husband. But in Africa and parts of Asia where divorce is easy she may not stay married long. Where divorce is more difficult, many women are not married since everywhere men tend to marry much younger women and the population growth has produced increasingly larger younger generations. Thus, single women and divorcees migrate to the cities. In Dahomey surveys indicated that from 25 to 30% of women living in town were on their own, while in Ethiopia, women outnumber men in the towns due to a high divorce rate. In Latin America, young women seek domestic service in towns and also migrate in larger numbers than men. Single untrained women have few options in urban settings; domestic service and prostitution are often mentioned as primary forms of employment. A large number of shop assistants in Latin America are also women. Others fit into the uncounted interstices of the economy. They buy a pack of cigarettes and sell them one at a time. They cook food and hawk it on the street. Men, too, engage in this informal sector. Statistics show, however, that male migrants usually progress from this sector into the statistically enumerated "modern sector" while women tend to remain uncounted, but working at these marginal jobs. Similarly, the exchange of services, which recent studies on America have shown permeates society from lower through middle class, goes uncounted. Women are more likely than men to do the exchanging, often doing child care or nursing. But men paint houses, fix cars, and exchange other such services. None of this economic activity enters into that mythical standard, the GNP, in America or in developing countries.

72

Besides trading, selling, or working in homes, many women become "walk-about-women"—prostitutes, femmes libres—something between a geisha and a call girl, or a mistress. Since polygamy is still more or less acceptable in Africa, mistresses often become "second wives." Such an arrangement may be secret; but it also may be honored by a declaration ceremony which has social if not legal, meaning. Since laws requiring monogamy have been passed in most countries the second wife's position is more precarious now than under customary law. Because bearing children can give the second wife a stronger claim on her husband, such liaisons lead to high fertility. More men have multiple wives in areas where women work than in those where women are kept in seclusion (Pool 1972:250). The cost of polygyny has tended to limit its continuance in cities to the middle and upper classes. Lower classes both in Africa and Indonesia tend to have only one wife at a time, but ease of divorce allows for frequent changes of partner. Economic independence of women and the phenomena of multiple liaisons seem to go hand in hand.

Interestingly, many market women in Africa argue in favor of polygyny. A survey conducted in the Ivory Coast in the 1960's found that 85% of the women came out in favor of polygyny! According to observers the women believe that in a monogamous marriage power accrues to the man as head of the household whereas formerly both men and women had to defer to the head of the lineage. Further, co-wives share the burden of household work and cooking, one woman could go off trading while another stayed home.

Such sharing is an anathema to the educated woman who strongly supports monogamy. Thus, the urban pattern of "illegal" polygyny includes dual households. Women-headed households therefore abound in much of Africa and in East London as well. Throughout Latin America and the Caribbean, a pattern of serial liaisons is typical. Indeed studies suggest that women purposely select different fathers for their children so that the potential support network for her and her children is enlarged (Stack 1974).

Middle and Upper Class Women

In contrast to the average woman in subsistence societies, the educated woman has adopted western values along with her western education and language. Nursing and teaching are considered suitable occupations for respectable women especially in countries where segregation continues so that demand for women teachers remains constant. Other occupations in the modern sector remain the purview of men. Thus, many educated women lose their economic independence and are forced to depend more on their husbands whose authoritarianism is reinforced (Gugler 1972:298). As a result more educated African women become militantly feminist (Dobert 8). Yet one highly placed female Ghanaian government servant argued to me that such activity was only for the housewife; she was too busy working to worry about feminism.

In Southeast Asia, the men dominate the bureaucracies and military, but commerce is open to women. In Jakarta, wives of the upper civil servants run shops and make jewelry. In Thailand, several large hotels are owned and run by women. Philippine women are adept in real estate, as stockbrokers, or running businesses; today in the Philippines more women than men attend private schools, a clear indicator of the value placed on women's ability to learn and to earn. Yet these women of Southeast Asia appear to us to be gentle and highly feminine.

Hoskins (n.d.) in her study of the Vietnamese women, explains this seeming contradiction. Women in Vietnam have traditionally been seen as pivotal to the family. Any activity which ensures the continuity or aids in the comfort of her family is acceptable. In the rural area she farmed or traded; in cities she responds to opportunity. With long years of war the bureaucracy was opened to women; such equality is a reassertion of traditional values which were overlayed both by the Chinese and French influences. Since economic activity is expected and accepted, Vietnamese women do not need to appear as men. Indeed, because the traditional roles of men were more narrowly defined, they have had more difficulty in adapting themselves to the urban scene. Also, because women are assumed to be working to benefit their family, there is no assumption on the part of male co-workers that the women are sexually available, a factor of great annoyance to many African women as it is to women in the United States.

Women in West Asia are least likely to work outside their homes. Islam requires men to protect and support the women in their family so that despite divorce, their women are supported. Still divorced women are somewhat more likely to work than married. Nonetheless the ideal is not to work and, if achieved, is considered a part of upward mobility. So local customs reinforce western stereotypes of women's roles into her place: the home.

Upper class women in most countries are less restricted by social norms than is the middle class. For example, in the United States, when only 2% of the age group went to college during the decade 1910-20, there was a higher percentage of women in professional and technical positions than there has been since. Similarly, even where women were kept in isolation, upper class women were often well-educated. Freed from household duties by servants, an occasional woman leader had emerged from this unpromising background to amaze the world. The two women prime ministers of India and Sri Lanka are examples of the phenomenon. Yet in both those countries, the rise in educational opportunities for the middle class has already reduced opportunities for the educated woman. When there is a surplus of college graduates and a scarcity of jobs, women are last hired, first fired.

Development is undercutting the elite women in yet another way. Independence and modernization have been accompanied by expanding administrative military bureaucracies. Fewer professionals remain independent of government. Nowhere are such bureaucracies receptive to women. Thus, fewer and fewer independent professionals, women or men, maintain visibility in these bureaucratized countries.

Summary and Implication

Development in the contemporary context means economic change in the pre-industrial societies. Even the terms, such as pre-industrial, underdeveloped, etc., imply an ordered series of stages through which any economy/country will pass. While in college courses we seek alternative models for development, western aid-givers have not until quite recently questioned their model. The declaration of the New International Economic Order or the Charter of Economic Rights and Duties, both initiated by the countries of the developing world, may be precurser of newer models yet. Unfortunately, there is little indication that the champions of the new economic order will be any more sensitive to women's needs than are the present western leaders.

A better understanding of the development process and its impact on women is needed. Any theory of women's changing roles and status would have to include many variables. Certainly women in nuclear or small family units which functioned as economic units play a stronger role than women who are economically dependent. While in the developed world there is an apparent return to the nuclear family, the division of labor which puts men into the public remunerative sphere, but leaves women with the private sphere which receives little or no economic reward, encourages dependence. In contrast, women in women-headed households or in polygynous marriages are forced to continue economic independence. Thus family type is not alone predictive of women's status. Still the trend in the United States is toward a nuclear family with mutually dependent partners, each with an income and with household responsibilities. We may be closer to the hunters and gatherers than we think! The very sensitivity of American women to their dependency fostered a concern over the impact of United States aid abroad. It is clear that if women in developing countries are not to fall prey to western development then aid givers must be sensitized to contemporary rules of women in each country in order to buttress or improve rather than bypass or undercut them.

Testimony on this subject before Congressional committees led to the formulation of the Percy Amendment to the Foreign Assistance Act of 1973 which requires the review of all United States aid projects to see how they affect the integration of women into the economics of their country. To implement this amendment, AID has established a special section of the AID administrators office which reviews all projects. So successful has this amendment been in raising the issue within the AID bureaucracy that Percy extended this idea to multi-lateral agencies receiving U.S. funds with an amendment to the present Foreign Assistance Act. Resolutions stressing the importance of recognizing women's contribution to development and of reviewing programs to see their impact on women have been introduced during 1974 at the world conference on population and food and at the UNESCO biennial meeting. Percy himself added a resolution in the General Assembly's third committee in December while in January the UNDP adopted a strong series of resolutions.

This flurry of official activity is being mirrored by an increase in research being done on the topic around the world. Women's studies have suddenly become legitimate outside the field of anthropology. The final success of the concern would be to have women's roles so much a recognized part of development that separate studies and resolutions would not be necessary. But in English the general term "he" has too often become a limited sexual description. For a time, to correct that bias, we need to continually remind developers that women's roles and employment are a vital part of development.[1]

---

[1] The Rural Development Network Bulletin No. 6, available from the Overseas Liaison Committee of the American Council on Education (1 DuPont Circle, Washington, D.C. 20036) focuses on "Women in Rural Development" and includes (1) a selected and annotated bibliography; (2) research projects and proposals; (3) innovative development programs and projects; and (4) a listing of seminars, symposia, and workshops.

REFERENCES

Albert, Ethel
1971   "Women of Burundi: A Study of Social Values" in Denise Paulme, ed., *Women of Tropical Africa* (Berkeley and Los Angeles: University of California Press), 179-216.

Aruri, Nassar Hasan
1972   *Jordan: A Study in Political Development* (The Hague: Nijhoff).

Bardhan, Pranab K.
1974   "On Life and Death Questions," *Economic and Political Weekly*, 1923.

Barkow, Jerome
1972   "Hausa Women and Islam" in Audrey Wipper, ed., *The Roles of African Women*, *The Canadian Journal of African Studies* 6, 2, 317-328.

Benston, Margaret
1969   "The Political Economy of Women's Liberation," *Monthly Review* 24, 1, 13-26.

Blake, Judith
1974   "The Changing Status of Women in Developed Countries," *Scientific American* 231, 3, 137-147.

Boaks, Kay
1974   "The Politics of Cultural Liberation" in Jane S. Jaquette, ed., *Women in Politics* (New York: Wiley), 322-342.

Boserup, Ester
1970   *Woman's Role in Economic Development* (London: George Allen and Unwin).

Boserup, Ester, and Christina Liljencrantz
1975   *Integration of Women in Development* (New York: United Nations Development Programme).

Castro, Fidel

    1974   "The Revolution has in Cuban women today an impressive political force", *Editorial de Ciencies Sociales*, La Habana.

Chaney, Elsa M.

    1973   "Women in Latin American Politics: The Case of Peru and Chile" in Ann Pescatello, Ed., *Female and Male in Latin America* (Pittsburgh: University of Pittsburgh Press), 103-139.

    1974   "The Mobilization of Women in Allende's Chile" in Jane S. Jaquette, ed., *Women in Politics* (New York: Wiley), 267-280.

Chessler, Phyllis P.

    1971   "Patient and Patriarch: Women in the Psychotherapeutic Relationship," in Vivian Gornick and Barbara Moran, eds., *Woman in Sexist Society* (New York: Basic Books, Inc.), 362-392.

Chodorow, Nancy

    1974   "Family Structure and Feminine Personality" in Michelle Zimbalist Rosaldo and Louise Lamphere, eds., *Women, Culture and Society* (Stanford: Stanford University Press), 43-66.

Coppinger, Robert M., and Paul C. Rosenblatt

    1968   "Romantic Love and Subsistence Dependence of Spouses," *Southwestern Journal of Anthropology* 24, 310-319.

Cordell, Magda, and John McHale with Guy Streetfield

    1975   *Women in World Terms: Facts and Trends* (Binghamton, N.Y.: Center for Integrative Studies, State University of New York).

Dobert, Margarita

    1970   "Liberation and the Women of Guinea," *Africa Report*, 15, 7, 26-28.

Douglas, Mary

    1966   *"Purity and Danger* (New York: Praeger).

Dumond, Don E.

    1975   "The Limitation of Human Population: A Natural History," *Science* 187, 713-722.

Dupire, Marguerite

1971   "The Position of Women in a Pastoral Society" in Denise Paulme, ed., *Women of Tropical Africa* (Berkeley and Los Angeles: University of California Press), 47-92.

Ebihara, May

1974   "Khmer Village Women in Cambodia" in Carol Mathiasson, ed., *Many Sisters* (New York: Free Press), 305-348.

Epstein, Scarlett

1959   "A Sociological Analysis of Witch Beliefs in a Mysore Village," in John Middleton, ed., *Magic, Witchcraft and Curing* (New York: Natural History Press).

Feminist Press

1976   *Portraits of Chinese Women* (Old Westbury, N.Y.: Feminist Press).

Fortes, Meyer

1954   "A Demographic Field Study in Ashanti" in Frank Lorimer, ed., *Culture and Human Fertility* (Switzerland: UNESCO).

Fox, Godfrey

1973   "Honor, Shame, and Women's Liberation in Cuba: Views of Working-Class Emigre Men" in Ann Pescatello, ed., *Female and Male in Latin America* (Pittsburgh: University of Pittsburgh Press), 273-292.

Friedl, Ernestine

1967   "The Position of Women: Appearance and Reality," *Anthropological Quarterly*, 40, 3, 97-108.

1975   *Women and Men: An Anthropological View* (New York: Holt, Rinehart and Winston).

Geertz, Hilda

1961   *The Javanese Family* (New York: Free Press).

Gordon, David

1968   *Women of Algeria: An Essay on Change* (Cambridge: Harvard Middle East Monograph Series).

Gugler, Josef

1972   "The Second Sex in Town" in Audrey Wipper, ed., *The Roles of African Women, The Canadian Journal of African Studies* 6, 2, 289-302.

Hammond, Dorothy, and Alta Jablow

1973　*Women: Their Economic Role in Traditional Societies*　(Reading, Mass.: Addison-Wesley Module in Anthropology, No. 35

Harris, Marvin

1971　*Culture, Man and Nature: An Introduction to General Anthropology*　(New York: Crowell).

Hogbin, Ian

1970　*The Island of Menstruating Men* (Scranton, Pa.: Chandler).

Hoskins, Marilyn

n.d.　"Vietnamese Women in a Changing Society" Mimeo.

Iglitzin, Lynne B., and Ruth Ross

1976　*Women in the World: A Comparative Study* (Santa Barbara, California: ABC-CLIO).

Jacquette, Jane S., ed.

1974　*Women in Politics* (New York: Wiley).

Jancar, Barbara

1974　"Women under Communism" in Jane S. Jaquette, ed., *Women in Politics* (New York: Wiley), 217-242.

Janeway, Elizabeth

1971　*Man's World, Woman's Place* (New York: Morrow).

Kaufman, Susan Purcell

1973　"Modernizing Women for a Modern Society: The Cuban Case" in Ann Pescatello, ed., *Female and Male in Latin America* (Pittsburgh: University of Pittsburgh Press), 257-272.

Lapidus, Gail Warshofsky

1974　"Modernization Theory and Sex Roles in Critical Perspective: The Case of the Soviet Union" in Jane S. Jacquette, ed., *Women in Politics* (New York: Wiley), 243-256.

Leader, Shelah Gilbert

1973　"The Emancipation of Chinese Women," *World Politics* 26, 55-79.

Leavitt, Ruby R.

1975　*Women Cross-Culturally* (Chicago: Aldine).

Lewis, I. M.

1971　*Ecstatic Religion: An Anthropological Study of Spirit Possession and Shamanism* (Harmondsworth: Penguin Books).

Lindenbaum, Shirley

1968   "Woman and the Left Hand: Social Status and Symbolism in East Pakistan," *Mankind* 6, 11, 537-544.

1975   *The Value of Women* (East Lansing: Michigan State University. South Asia Series, Occasional Paper No. 23).

n.d.   "A Wife is the Hand of Man" *Anthropological Studies: Sex Roles in the New Guinea Highlands.* (In Press).

Little, Kenneth

1973   *African Women in Towns* (Cambridge: Cambridge University Press).

Mandelbaum, David

1973   *Fertility in India* (Berkeley: University of California Press).

Maranda, Elli Kongas

1974   "Lau, Malaita: A Woman is an Alien Spirit" in Carolyn Matthiasson, ed., *Many Sisters* (New York: Free Press), 177-202.

Matthiasson, Carolyn

1974   *Many Sisters: Women in Cross-Cultural Perspective* (New York: Free Press).

McWilliams, Nancy

1974   "Contemporary Feminism, Consciousness-Raising, and Changing Views of the Political" in Jane S. Jacquette, ed., *Women in Politics* (New York: Wiley), 157-170.

Metha, Rama

1970   *The Western Educated Hindu Woman* (Bombay: Asia Publishing House).

Mintz, Sidney W.

1971   "Men, Women and Trade," *Comparative Studies Society and History* 13, 247-269.

Murdock, George P., and Caterina Provost

1973   "Factors in the Division of Labour by Sex: A Cross-Cultural Analysis," *Ethnology* 12, 2, 203-225.

Nadel, S. F.

1942   *Black Byzantium* (Cambridge: Cambridge University Press).

1952   "Witchcraft in Four African Societies: An Essay in Comparison," *American Anthropologist* 54, 18-29.

Newman, Lucile F.

    1972   *Birth Control: An Anthropological View* (Reading, Mass.: Addison-Wesley Module in Anthropology No. 27).

Oakley, Ann

    1972   *Sex, Gender and Society* (New York: Harper and Row).

O'Barr, Jean

    1970   *Ten-House Cells and Their Leaders: Micropolitics in Pare District, Tanzania.* (Unpublished Ph.D. thesis, Northwestern University, Evanstan, Illinois).

    1975   "Making the Invisible Visible: African Women in Politics and Policy" in Nancy Hafkin and Edna Bay, eds., *African Women in Changing Perspective, African Studies Review* xv III, 3, 19-27.

Ocloo, Esther

    1974   "The Ghanian Market Woman," Paper prepared for Society for International Development 14th World Conference, Abidjon.

Ortner, Sherry B.

    1974   "Is Female to Male as Nature is to Culture?" in Michelle Zimbalist Rosaldo and Louise Lamphere, eds.k *Women, Culture and Society* (Stanford: Stanford University Press), 67-88.

Overseas Liaison Committee

    1976   "Women in Rural Development," special issue of *Rural Development Bulletin* (OLC, American Council on Education, 1 DuPont Circle, Washington, D.C. 20036).

Papanek, Hannah

    1973   "Purdah: Separate Worlds and Symbolic Shelter," *Comparative Studies in Sociology and History,* 50, 3.

Paulme, Denise

    1971   *"Women of Tropical Africa* (Berkeley: University of California Press).

Pescatello, Ann

    1973   *Female and Male in Latin America* (Pittsburgh: Pittsburgh University Press).

Pool, Janet

    1972   "A Cross-Comparative Study of Aspects of Conjugal Behavior Among Women of Three West African Countries" in Audrey Wipper, ed., *The Roles of African Women, The Canadian Journal of African Studies* 6, 2, 233-260.

Raphael, Dana
  1975   *Being Female: Reproduction, Power and Change* (Chicago: Aldine).

Remy, Dorothy
  n.d.   "Underdevelopment and the Experience of Women: A Zania Case Study," in S. D. Osoba and G. P. Williams, eds., *Nigeria: Economy and Society* in press).

Remy, Dorothy, and John Weeks
  1973   "Employment, Occupation and Inequality in a Non-Industrialized City" in K. Wolmuth, ed., *Employment in Emerging Societies* (New York: Praeger).

Rosaldo, Michelle Zimbalist
  1974   "Women, Culture, and Society: A Theoretical Overview" in Michelle Zimbalist Rosaldo and Louise Lamphere, eds., *Women, Culture and Society* (Stanford: Stanford University Press), 17-42.

Rosaldo, Michelle Zimbalist, and Louise Lamphere
  1974   *"Women, Culture, and Society* (Stanford: Stanford University Press).

Rosenblatt, Paul C., and Paul C. Cosby
  1972   "Courtship Patterns Associated with Freedom of Choice of Spouse," *Journal of Marriage and the Family* 34, 639-695.

Rostow, Walt
  1960   *The Stages of Economic Growth* (New York: Cambridge University Press).

Rowbotham, Sheila
  1974   *Women, Resistance and Revolution* (New York: Vintage).

Sacks, Karen
  1974   "Engels Revisited: Women, the Organization of Production, and Private Property" in Michelle Zimbalist Rosaldo and Louise Lamphere, eds., *Women, Culture and Society* (Stanford: Stanford University Press), 207-222.

Salaff, Janet Weitzner and Judith Merkle
  1971   "Women in Revolution: The Lessons of the Soviet Union and China," *Berkeley Journal of Sociology*, 166-191

Sanday, Peggy R.
  1973   "Toward a Theory of the Status of Women," *American Anthropologist* 75:1682-1700.

1974   "Female Status in the Public Domain" in Michelle Zimbalist Rosaldo and Louise Lamphere, eds., *Women, Culture and Society* (Stanford: Stanford University Press), 189-206.

Schneider, Jane

1971   "Of Vigilance and Virgins: Honor, Shame and Access to Resources in Mediterranean Societies," *Ethnology* 9, 1, 1-24.

Scott, Hilda

1974   *Does Socialism Liberate Women: Experiences from Eastern Europe* (Boston: Beacon Press).

Simmons, Emmy Bartz

1974   "Cultural Assumptions and Women's Roles in Development," paper prepared for Society for International Development 14th World Conference, Abidjan.

Stack, Carol

1974   *All Our Kin* (New York: Harper and Row).

Sullerot, Evelyne

1971   *Women, Society and Change* (New York: McGraw Hill World University Library).

Tinker, Irene, and Michele Bo Bransen, eds.

1976   *Women in Development* (Washington: Overseas Development Council, 1717 Massachusetts Ave., N.W. 20036).

Trey, J. E.

1972   "Women in the War Economy—World War II," *The Review of Radical Political Economics* 4, 3, 41-57.

Van Allen, Judith

1974a   "Women in Africa: Modernization Means More Dependency," *The Center Magazine.* May-June, 60-67.

1974b   *"Memsahib, Militents, Femme Libre:* Political and Apolitical Styles of Modern African Women" in Jane S. Jaquette, ed., *Women in POLitics* (New York: Wiley), 304-321.

1975   " 'Aba Riots' or Ibgo 'Women's War'?—Ideology, Stratification and the Invisibility of Women" in Nancy Hafkin and Edna Bay, *African Women in Changing Perspective, African Studies Review.* forthcoming.

Vinogradov, Amal
 1974   "French Colonialism as Reflected in the Male-Female Interaction in Morocco," *Transactions of the New York Academy of Sciences*, Series II, 35, 2, 192-199.

Ward, Barbara
 1963   *Women in the New Asia* (Paris: UNESCO).

Wipper, Audrey (ed.)
 1972   *The Roles of African Women, Canadian Journal of African Studies* 6,2 (special issue).

Yang, C. K.
 1965   *The Chinese Family in the Communist Revolution* (Cambridge, Mass.:   M.I.T. Press).

Youssef, Nadia H.
 1974   *Women and Work in Developing Countries* (Berkeley, California: Institute of International Studies Population Monograph Series No. 15, University of California).

SELECTED BIBLIOGRAPHIES ON THIRD WORLD WOMEN

African Studies Centre, Cambridge

  1974   *African Women: A Select Bibliography.* 76 pp.

Available from African Studies Center, Sidgwick Avenue, Cambridge, England. No charge.

Indexed by both country and subject; entries cover development studies, economics, elites, family, legal position, ornamentation, politics, religion and ritual, sexual relations, urban studies, women's organizations, youth.

Buvinic, Mayra

  1975   *Women in Development: Annotated Bibliography of Published and Unpublished Studies.* 150 pp.

Available from Overseas Development Council, 1717 Massachusetts Ave., NW, Washington, D.C. 20036 / (202) 234-8701. $2.50

Prepared as a working document for AAAS Seminar on Women in Development which preceeded Mexico City IWY meeting in June 1975. Extensive annotations of manuscripts organized according to nine subject categories, each of which will be preceded by an introduction characterizing the studies available in that segment of the field (general; women's roles and status; women's behavioral patterns; women's legal and political participation; women's organizations and communciations networks; women in rural settings; women in urban settings; education, occupation and employment; and nutrition, health and family planning). Each subject category will be subdivided according to geographic focus (multiregional and cross-cultural, Latin America and Caribbean, Africa, North Africa and Middle East, Asia and Pacific, North America and Europe).

Birdsall, Nancy

  1973   *Annotated Bibliography,* Vol. 2, No. 1. 39 pp.

Available from Interdisciplinary Communications Program, Smithsonian Institution: Washington, D.C. 20036. No charge.

An introduction to the social science literature on "woman's place" and fertility in the developing world.

Gulick, John, and Margaret E. Gulick

1974   *An Annotated Bibliography of Sources Concerned with Women in the Modern Muslim Middle East. Princeton Near East Paper*, No. 17. 26 pp.

Available through the Program in Near Eastern Studies, Princeton University, Princeton, N.J. 08540. $1.00

Jacobs, Sue-Ellen

1974   *Women in Perspective – A Guide for Cross-Cultural Studies.* 299 pp.

Available from University of Illinois Press, Urbana, Illinois 61801. $3.45.

Indexed by geographical area (Africa, Middle East, Asia, Europe, Oceania, South America and North America) and by subject (general references, primate studies; anatomy and physiology; psychological studies; sex and sexuality; socialization; role development and child-rearing practices; family, marriage, kinship, residence, and divorce; homosexuality; menstruation, pregnancy, abortion; prostitution; women and religion; women in prison; political roles, power, legal status of women (includes matriarchy); economics and employment; education; women and war; misogyny; women in history; suffrage, historical feminism; modern feminism; women in literature; mythology, and folk tradition; miscellaneous classics; biographies and auto-biographies; futurism, utopianism; bibliographies; publications of women's studies, collectives and centers; publications useful for dealing with sex discrimination.

Knaster, Meri

1976   *Annotated bibliography on women in Mexico, Central America and the Spanish Caribbean.* In process of revision and updating to encompass the South American countries as well.

Available from Center for Latin American Studies, Stanford University, Palo Alto, California 94305. No information on price.

Perlman, M., and M. P. Moal

1971   "Analytical Bibliography" in Denise Paulme, ed., *Women of Tropical Africa* (University of California Press: Berkeley and Los Angeles), pp. 231-294. $3.65.

Citations drawn from anthropological literature covering social and legal status, family life, initiation, women's associations, work, ornaments, political activities, ritual functions, education and emancipation, schools, adult education.

Raghaven, Susheila

1974   Women's role and development policies, a bibliographic index. 8 pp. Reproduction charge.

Available from Committee on Women in Development, Society for International Development, 1346 Connecticut Avenue, N.W., Washington, D.C. 20036.

Women's Studies Abstracts

Quarterly publication which abstracts materials on women and their interests and lists other articles and books on these subjects. P. O. Box 1, Rush, New York 14543. (First volume published in 1972).

INFORMATION ON FILMS

I. Film series dealing specifically with third world women

A. *Women Today: Tradition and Change*

Six in a series of 27 color documentaries produced by the American Universities Field Staff are devoted entirely to women.

1. WOMEN IN A CHANGING WORLD 48 min.
Focus: Perceptions of Roles and Status
Location: China Coast, Northern Kenya, Bolivia, Afghanistan

All over the world, centuries of tradition are being challenged and changed by new opportunities created through education, and by pressures for economic, social, and political equality. At the same time, discrimination against women continues.

In this film women from four diverse cultures express their concern with fundamental rights and human dignity as it affects their individual lives.

2. AFGHAN WOMEN 17 min.
Focus: Religious and Social Tradition
Location: Rural Afghanistan

Afghan women live separated from public life, in keeping with conservative Islamic tradition. The film follows their daily routine, demonstrating their limited, yet influential, roles. Through the words and lives of these women, we observe the serenity of communal sisterhood.

3. ANDEAN WOMEN 19 min.
Focus: Indian family life, traditional women's roles
Location: Rural Bolivia

This colorful view of the peasant woman's daily life is filmed against the starkly beautiful background of the Andean highlands. These Indian women carry much of the responsibility for the farm family's survival, yet, paradoxically, their world is dominated by men.

4. BORAN WOMEN 18 min.
   Focus: Equality, change, education
   Location: Herding group in Northern Kenya

   Boran women wield power in their society through their control over
   the distribution of foodstuffs. The film shows women at the diverse
   tasks: fetching water from great distances, caring for children, homemaking, and homebuilding, while the men manage the herds. An older
   women expresses a provocative perspective on change.

5. THREE ISLAND WOMEN 17 min.
   Focus: Equality, different generational views
   Location: Soko Island, Hong Kong Territorial Waters

   Three Chinese women ages 21, 34, and 84, agree that life is better for
   them now than in the past. In this changing society, men and women
   are considered equal, and we see women doing hard physical labor.
   They discuss their role in decision-making: "In the past, husbands
   were almighty—it's not that way anymore . . . ."

6. A CHINESE FARM WIFE 17 min.
   Focus: Equality, changing family life
   Location: Rural Taiwan

   A collection of informative glimpses into the varied life of Mrs. Li, a
   housewife and mother who manages the family farm and works in the
   rice fields. She also takes an active part in community activities such as
   a cooking contest, preparation for her daughter's marriage, and other
   ritual celebrations.

7. For further information: Fieldstaff Films
                                3 Lebanon Street
                                Hanover, New Hampshire 03755
                                (603) 643-2110

B. *Womanpower*

The United Nations has produced three color films on women which relate
to the themes of International Women's Year

1. *WOMANPOWER: Equality and Development*
   (Tunisia) 30 min. No. 161

This film examines development and its relationship to the changing status of women. At the first International Women's Forum convened by the United Nations we hear delegates from all over the world speak out on conditions in their own countries—and they find remarkable similarities. Issues raised at the Forum are illustrated through a visit to Tunisia, where the Personal Status Code of 1956 granted women greater equality before the law. Today, more and more Tunisian women are joining the work force; family planning services are widely available, and abortion is legal and free. New national and international programs are needed to ensure full integration of women in the total development effort.

2. *WOMANPOWER: The People's Choice*
   (Columbia)   30 min.   No. 162

   To influence as well as to share in economic and social development, women must hold political office and participate in the law-making process. In Colombia, a country where women were given the right to vote in 1957, this film follows the struggle of three women running for election: for the first time in Latin America, a contending party candidate to the presidency is a women; with full support of her district, a mother of seven is campaigning to be re-elected to a third term in the Bogota City Council; in office since 1957, "the senator," is re-elected . . . the only one of our three candidates who wins her campaign.

3. *WOMANPOWER: A Woman's Place is . . .*
   (Sri Lanka and Sweden)   30 min.   No. 163

   This film explores the changing role of women in political, economic, and social development in two very different countries Sri Lanka and Sweden.

   In Sri Lanka, Madame Bandaranaike is Prime Minister, and she has included women as an essential part of the labor force for her new mechanized agricultural program. With an economy based on agriculture, women in Sri Lanka are also urged to enroll in intensive farming studies, and to work together in cooperatives. But before women can assume these new responsibilities, their traditional roles must first change as we see happening in Sweden. Roles are not changed simply by hiring women as machine operators in a steel factory, but by a basic revision in social conditioning. A conscious effort is being made in Sweden to erase sex role stereotyping as transmitted to children in the home and at school.

91

4. The distributor in the United States for these films is:

       FMS Films
       P. O. Box 7316
       Alexandria, Va. 22307
       (703)768-3912

C. *Women in Development*

UNDP, in co-operation with the UN Secretariat for International Women's Year and non-governmental organizations, has produced a multi-media packet entitled, "Women in Development," which explores local planning efforts.

The packet includes two 16mm color films; six, 35 mm color slide albums with audio-cassettes (in English); texts in English, French and Spanish, as well as background reports and study guides.

Designed for use within the UN development system, and by governmental and non-governmental agencies, the packet brings to audiences a vivid "presence" of women in many developing countries facing the issues on their own terms.

The materials are for orientation and training sessions for workers in public health, rural and vocational training, community organizations, cottage industries, retailing, animal husbandry, inter-agency co-operation, small technology, financing and credit for rural women and fertility. Some items will also be valuable for general interest groups and could be used selectively for television.

The packet was first created through joint financing by the Non-Governmental Organizations Tribune at the World Conference on International Women's Year in July, 1975, the American Association for the Advancement of Science, and UNDP's Division of Information. It also includes a slide-sound album by World Education, Inc.

The contents include:

1. *Outside GNP,* 16 mm color film, nine minutes. Explains that women's labor in subsistence agriculture and in the home is excluded from gross national product figures and shows what this deletion means to the planner, to the whole of society and to women in particular.

2. *Overview: Development and Women*, about 80 color slides, audio-cassette, 10 minutes. Answers the question—What kind of development?—by showing that to increase consumer goods at the expense of social development fails to improve the quality of life for all.

3. *Honduras: Community Awareness for Development*, Slide-sound, 10 minutes. Takes the viewers step-by-step along with planners and members of a small community as they assess priority problems and decide how to solve them.

4. *Ethiopia: A New Education in Family Life*, slide-sound, 10 minutes. Shows how a national NGP for women integrated training in economic activities and health services in their family-life education projects.

5. *Economic Commission for Africa: Seeking New Planners*, slide-sound, 10 minutes. Presents the ECA's approach to women and development that resulted from studies of co-operative ventures in Kenya that independent women's groups had implemented themselves.

6. *Philippines: "Self-Actualizing" Education*, slide-sound, 10 minutes. Illustrates how well women are aware of their economic needs and how readily they can be motivated by non-formal education to address those needs.

7. *Small Technology: New Tools for Women*, slide-sound, 10 minutes. Shows the importance of small technologies to women in developing countries, how improvements could offer relief, and points to ways of improving accessibility to better tools.

8. *Inside GNP* (working title), 16mm film, 23 minutes. Shows several examples in Colombia of women assuming improved roles in the economy, and innovative links between planners and community participants.

9. *Literature.* Scripts of the sound tracks, additional reference notes and study guides tailored to each of the above audio-visual presentations.

10. To order, write Women in Development Multi-Media Packet, U. N. Development Programme, U. N. Plaza, N.Y. 10017.

II. General sources of information on films about women

A. *PROJECT ON THE STATUS OF WOMEN AND EDUCATION OF WOMEN* OF THE AMERICAN ASSOCIATION OF COLLEGES (1818 R Street, N.W., Washington, D.C. 20009) published *Women and Film: A Resource Handbook* which is available upon request from them. This 26 page booklet lists films by topic; a few are on third world countries. In the booklet they list sources for further exploration.

B. *THE FILM CATALOGS OF AUDIO-VISUAL DEPARTMENTS* of major universities (especially at Indiana University, the University of Michigan, the University of California at Berkeley and the University of California at Los Angeles) are well indexed and contain entries under *women* and by country. *These catalogs are available either by writing directly to the schools or at the media/audio-visual center of colleges and universities.*

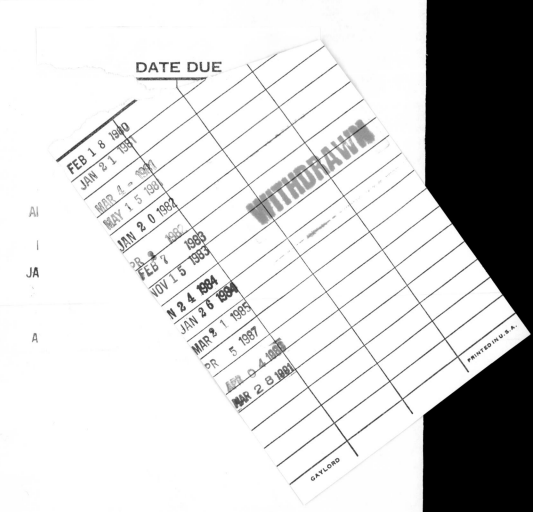